KT-214-571

A MACDONALD BOOK

Editor
Bridget Daly

Design
Sally Boothroyd

Production
Rosemary Bishop

© Macdonald & Co (Publishers) Ltd. 1984

First published in Great Britain in 1984
by Macdonald & Co (Publishers) Ltd
London and Sydney
A Pergamon Press plc Company

Reprinted in 1988
All rights reserved

Printed and bound by
New Interlitho s.p.a.
Milan, Italy

Macdonald & Co (Publishers Ltd)
Greater London House
Hampstead Road
London NW1 7QX

BRITISH LIBRARY CATALOGUING IN PUBLICATION DATA

Maryon-Davis, Alan
    Body facts.
    1. Man. Physiology For children
    I. Title   II. Kenyon, Tony
    612

    ISBN 0-356-09216-X
        0-356-16416-O Pbk

Spot the words in the book
which are printed in *italics*.
This means that Little Doc is
talking about a particular
picture on the page and
explaining what the picture is
showing.

BODY FACTS

by

Dr. Alan Maryon-Davis

Illustrated by Tony Kenyon

Macdonald

Body Basics

What is this book about?

It's about you and me and the rest of us human beings. It's about the human body and how it works. It's a book of fascinating facts about what you are and what makes you tick. For instance, did you know that when you sneeze, the air blasts through your nose at over 160 km per hour? Or that on an average day your heart works hard enough to lift you 300 metres up in the sky? Or that the inside surface of an adult man's lungs could cover the entire area of a tennis court?

I'm the Doc by the way. I'm going to take you on a guided tour of your body from top to toe, explaining this and that and cracking a few jokes if I can think of any. But first we must have a few maps. So on the next four pages we will look at the body's basic layout and see how the bits and pieces fit together.

A cell

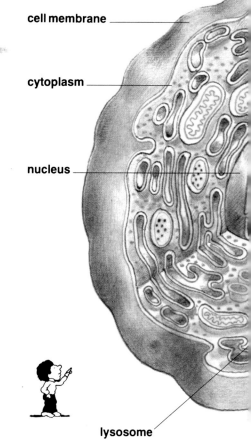

cell membrane

cytoplasm

nucleus

lysosome

What are we made of?

The human body is really incredibly complicated, like a huge bustling city. It has its own transport system for moving things around – the bloodstream or **circulatory system**. It has its telephone system for sending instant messages – the **nervous system**. It has its own factories for making chemicals – the glands in the **endocrine system**. It has drains for removing waste products – the **urinary system**. And so on.

Each system has a number of different parts to make it work and these are called **organs** (liver, stomach, heart etc.). Each organ contains different **tissues**, like muscle tissue so that it can squeeze and pull, or fatty tissue to store your fat. But all tissues have one thing in common if they are looked at under a microscope – they are all made of millions of very tiny capsules of living matter. These are called **cells**.

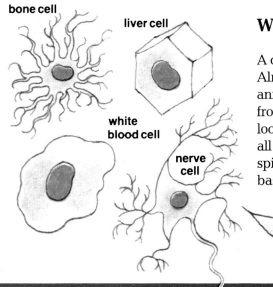

bone cell

liver cell

white blood cell

nerve cell

smooth muscle cell

What is a cell?

A cell is the basic unit of life. Almost all living things, plant and animal, are made of cells. Cells from different human tissues all look very different because they all have special jobs to do. But in spite of this they all have the same basic pattern or structure.

*The outer skin or **cell membrane** lets in oxygen and food substances and lets out carbon dioxide and waste products. The **cytoplasm** is a jelly-like material. The **nucleus** contains a tangle of 46 very important fine threads called **chromosomes**. These hold coded instructions (**genes**), which control the various jobs done by the other structures within the cell.*

How do cells multiply?

The human body contains about 75 trillion cells! All these have come from the single original cell that resulted from fertilisation of the mother's egg-cell by the father's sperm (see page 43).

The cell multiplies by dividing in two. Then these divide to make 4, 8, 16, 32 and so on. Cells are constantly dying and being replaced.

Nerve cells are unusual as they are not replaced. They start dying from the time we are about 18 onwards!

1 Each of the chromosomes makes an exact copy of itself. 2 The copies then move to the opposite side of the nucleus. 3 The nucleus then splits in two, separating the two sets of chromosomes. 4 The rest of the cell then divides in two, each half taking one nucleus. The result is two smaller cells with exactly the same coded instructions in their genes.

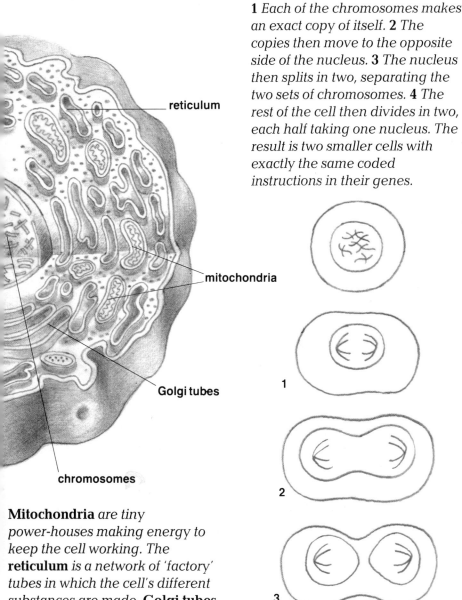

reticulum

mitochondria

Golgi tubes

chromosomes

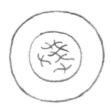
1

2

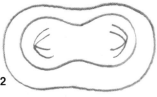
3

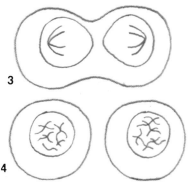
4

Mitochondria *are tiny power-houses making energy to keep the cell working. The* **reticulum** *is a network of 'factory' tubes in which the cell's different substances are made.* **Golgi tubes** *are where substances made in the factory tubes are stored, ready for 'export'.* **Lysosomes** *make enzymes (chemical substances) for digesting food.*

What we are made of

carbohydrates

iron

fats

protein

salt

other minerals

water

Fascinating facts

★ Nearly 60% of an adult man is water. That's about 40 litres, enough to fill 4 pairs of man-size wellington boots. His main tissues are:

muscle 43%	organs 12%
fat 14%	skin 9%
bone 14%	blood 8%

★ Skin cells only last about a week before they die. Red blood cells live for about 4 months. Bone cells last 10-30 years.

The skeletal system

A framework of about 200 bones and 100 joints makes a complicated system of props and levers. Your skeleton is essential for movement and breathing and to stop you collapsing in a soggy heap. It also protects delicate organs like the brain and heart. Bone is living tissue containing deposits of the mineral calcium. This gives it its great strength. The soft red marrow inside the larger bones is where blood cells are made. More about bones and joints on pages 33 and 46.

The muscular system

The body has about 650 muscles firmly anchored to your bones. Muscles are fleshy power-packs which enable you to move by pulling your bones and bending or straightening your joints. Muscles pull by getting shorter and fatter under orders from the brain. These orders are sent as electrical signals in 'motor' nerves. Muscles are the lean meat of your body, making 43% of your weight. More about muscles on page 32.

The nervous system

This is your body's telephone system. Your brain is the control centre; receiving signals from the sense organs, remembering what they mean, deciding what to do, and sending orders to the muscles. Your spinal cord is the main trunk route. And your nerves are the branching wires that connect with all parts of the body. **Sensory nerves** carry signals from the sense organs to the spinal cord and brain. **Motor nerves** carry orders to the muscles. More about the nervous system on page 14.

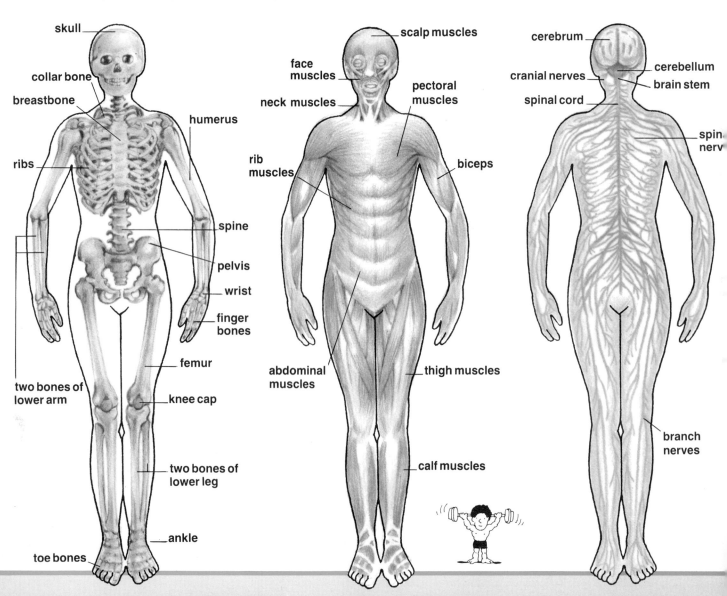

Skeletal system labels: skull, collar bone, breastbone, ribs, humerus, two bones of lower arm, spine, pelvis, wrist, finger bones, femur, knee cap, two bones of lower leg, ankle, toe bones

Muscular system labels: scalp muscles, face muscles, neck muscles, rib muscles, pectoral muscles, biceps, abdominal muscles, thigh muscles, calf muscles

Nervous system labels: cerebrum, cerebellum, brain stem, cranial nerves, spinal cord, spinal nerves, branch nerves

The circulatory and lymph systems

This is your body's transport system. Oxygen and food substances are carried to every cell by the blood which circulates around the body, streaming through the tissues in tiny pipes called **capillaries**. The heart pumps the blood along supply pipes, called **arteries**, to the lungs and other tissues. **Veins** bring blood back to the heart. There is a network of even tinier vessels which filter and drain excess fluid or **lymph** containing dead cells or bacteria from the tissues into a main vein near the heart. More about the circulation on page 30.

The respiratory system

Your body's ventilation system. Breathing air in and out gets vital oxygen into your blood and the waste product carbon dioxide out from it. Muscles work your ribcage and diaphragm to suck air into the **lungs**. It passes through your nose or mouth, **throat** (pharynx), **voice-box** (larynx), **windpipe** (trachea) and into the **air-tubes** (bronchi) of each lung. These end in hundreds of millions of tiny air balloons called **alveoli**, each wrapped in a mesh of capillaries. Oxygen and carbon dioxide can pass easily to and from the air in the alveoli and the blood in the capillaries. For more on breathing see page 26.

More about systems

Nervous system
Cerebrum is the decision-making part of the brain.
Cerebellum controls balance.
Brain stem controls functions like breathing and heart beat rate.
Cranial nerves control face, nose, eyes, mouth, ears, throat, (12 pairs).
Spinal cord is the main nerve line connecting spinal nerves to brain.
Spinal nerves are 31 pairs of nerves branching from spinal cord, dividing into more branches.
Branch nerves are branches of spinal nerves carrying messages to and from muscles and sense organs in skin, joints etc.

Circulation
Aorta is the main artery carrying blood with oxygen to the body.
Carotid arteries are the main arteries to the head.
Jugular veins are the main veins from the head.
Pulmonary artery takes dark blood to the lungs for oxygen.
Pulmonary veins bring blood with oxygen to the heart to be pumped.

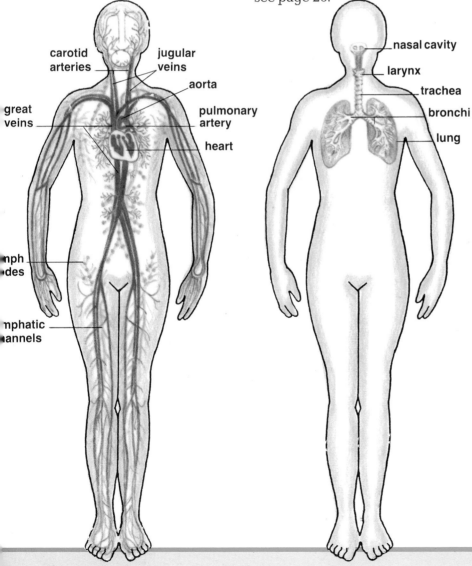

carotid arteries — jugular veins — aorta — great veins — pulmonary artery — heart — lymph nodes — lymphatic channels

nasal cavity — larynx — trachea — bronchi — lung

Fascinating facts

★ The fastest human muscle can make our eyelids blink at about 5 blinks a second. This is nothing compared to the muscles that work a midge's wings. *They* can beat at over 1000 times a second!

★ The heart beats about 70 times a minute on average. The total length of all the blood vessels in the body equals 96,000 km. That's nearly 2½ times around the world!

★ Your hand and wrist contain 27 bones!

The digestive system

This converts your food and drink into substances which can be used as fuel or building blocks by every cell in your body. After food is swallowed it is mixed with digestive juices in the **stomach**. It then passes into a very long coiled tube called the **intestine** where more juices are added. These turn the food into chemical substances which enter the bloodstream in the intestine wall. They then pass to the **liver** for more processing before being sent round the body in the circulation. Waste is expelled from the digestive system through the **anus**. More about the digestive system on page 36.

The urinary system

This removes waste products from the bloodstream and controls the amount of water in the body. Blood is filtered as it passes through the **kidneys**, making a constant trickle of unwanted water and waste products called **urine**. This passes down long pipes called **ureters** and is collected in a bag called the **bladder**. This empties by relaxing the **sphincter** (pinching) muscle, and squirting the urine out through a pipe called the **urethra**. A hormone from the pituitary gland controls the amount of urine produced. For more on the waterworks see page 38.

The hormone system

This is the 'postal system' sending instructions from one part of the body to another, using the bloodstream. The messengers are special chemical substances called **hormones**. There are many different hormones and they control many important processes in the body. Each hormone is made in an **endocrine gland** and 'posted' into the bloodstream. It circulates around the body and is delivered to whichever organ it is 'addressed' to. This organ is then turned on or off, or high or low, according to the endocrine gland's instructions.

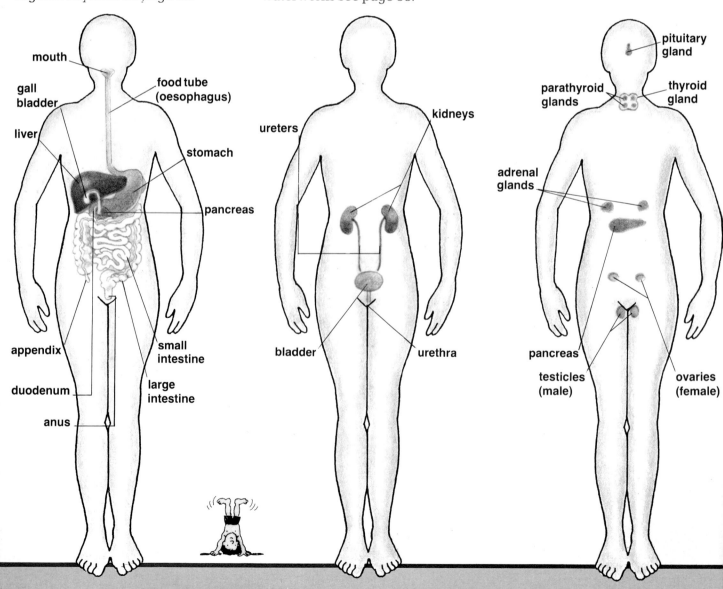

The reproductive systems

Men and women have different reproductive systems. The female sex organs are the **ovaries**, two ovals lying in the base of the abdomen. Close to each ovary are the funnel-shaped **fallopian tubes** which open into the **womb**. The womb opens into the passage to the outside world called the **vagina**. The male organs lie outside the body in a special bag called the **scrotum**. The system includes the **testicles**, **prostate gland**, **penis** and **sperm tubes**. The sex organs, or **testicles**, are a mass of sperm-producing tubes.

These **sperm**, or seeds, are the things that combine with the female **ova**, or eggs, (made in the ovaries) to make a baby. In sexual intercourse, sperm are placed in the woman's vagina and then swim through the womb to the fallopian tubes. There a sperm meets and fertilises the egg to make an **embryo** baby which develops in the womb. Nine months later the baby is born through the vagina and the woman's breasts start making milk to feed the baby with. For more on reproduction, see pages 40 to 44.

More about the hormone system

Pituitary gland is the 'master' gland in the base of the brain. It controls most of the other endocrine glands.
Thyroid gland produces the hormone thyroxin which controls the use of energy by all tissues, helps growth and development.
Parathyroid glands regulate the amount of calcium in the blood.
Adrenal glands produce many hormones including adrenalin which controls circulation and muscular action.
Pancreas produces the hormone insulin which controls the use of sugar in the body.
Testicles (male) produce the hormone tostesterone which controls sexual development and sperm production.
Ovaries (female) produce the hormones progesterone and oestrogen which prepare the womb for pregnancy.

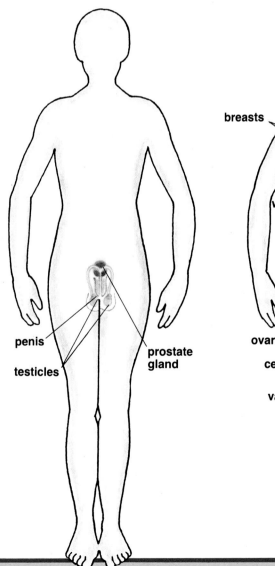

penis

testicles

prostate gland

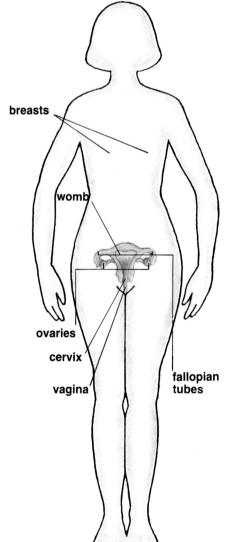

breasts

womb

ovaries

cervix

vagina

fallopian tubes

For more on reproduction, see pages 40 to 44.

Quiz
Complete the following sentences:
1) The heart is part of the _____ system.
2) We have __ bones in our hand and wrist.
3) In breathing, air is sucked into the _____ .

Pick out the right word for the following:
1) A blood vessel that carries blood back to the heart is a:
a) artery b) vein c) capillary.
2) Marrow is found in the:
a) muscles b) heart c) bones.
3) Sperm are made in the:
a) vagina b) penis c) testicles.

Hair

What is hair made of?

Hair consists of a very strong substance called **keratin** and each hair is made by special cells in a tiny pit in the skin called a **hair follicle**.

Pull out one of your hairs. Ouch! Now look at it under a magnifying glass. You will see white bits at the end which are the remains of the follicle cells. Hair always snaps in the follicle because that is where it is weakest. Further from the scalp it is much tougher. A hair is about 1/10 mm in diameter. Stroke a hair. You will find that it is smoother when stroked in one direction. This is because the hair has hundreds of ridges on its surface pointing away from the root. They help to keep dust and dirt out of the skin.

Hairs in the skin

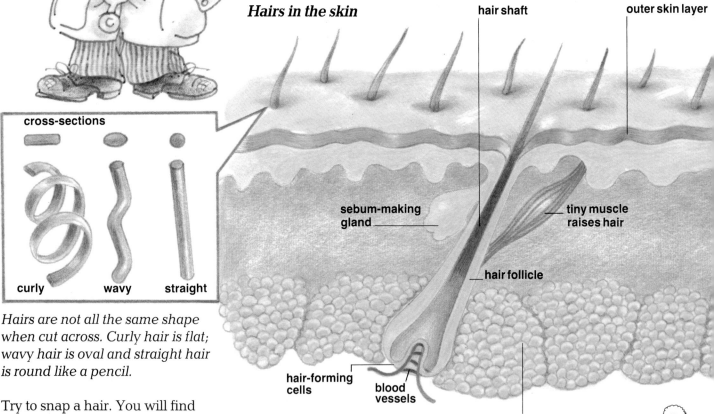

cross-sections

curly   wavy   straight

Hairs are not all the same shape when cut across. Curly hair is flat; wavy hair is oval and straight hair is round like a pencil.

hair shaft

outer skin layer

sebum-making gland

tiny muscle raises hair

hair follicle

hair-forming cells

blood vessels

fatty tissue

Try to snap a hair. You will find that it is incredibly tough for its size. Keratin is the same stuff that the outer layer of your skin and your nails are made of, and is very hard-wearing.

How does hair grow?

As new cells are produced in the hair follicle, the old ones become filled with keratin and die, forming a hair. So the hair gets pushed out by the new cells growing behind it rather like toothpaste out of a tube.

An adult's hair grows about a millimetre every three days or 12-13 cm a year. Each hair usually falls out after a few years' growth or about 1 metre in length. But some hairs fall out much shorter than that and some grow much longer.

What is hair for?

Hairs are able to trap a layer of air between them which helps to prevent the loss of heat from the body. That is why a fur coat is so warm. Hair can also protect the scalp from the burning rays of the sun. So it helps to keep our brains at an even temperature.

Why is hair different colours?

Like other cells in the skin, the hair-producing cells may contain a brown colouring matter (or pigment) called **melanin**. If so, the pigment appears in the hair as it grows. Hair which has a great deal of pigment is black or dark brown. Blond hair has little pigment and red hair has a medium amount. Mousey hair has a mixture of these types. White hair has no pigment at all.

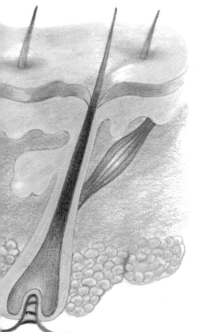

Why do men have beards?

At puberty, around the age of 13-15, the soft hairs on boys' cheeks, chins and upper lips become tougher and thicker and if they do not shave, a beard will grow. This happens because a special chemical in the blood, the male sex hormone **testosterone**, 'switches on' the hair follicles on the face. Many other changes also take place (see Growth page 44).

Why do some men go bald?

If you are a boy and your father is bald, then you too are likely to be bald when you are his age. People are not entirely sure why baldness occurs, except that it tends to run in families and has something to do with the male sex hormone.

Take a close look at a bald head with your magnifying glass (ask the owner first). You will see that there are still thousands of hairs over the bald area – but they are tiny, fine hairs.

What is dandruff?

White flecks which are clumps of skin cells from the surface of the scalp stuck together with a greasy substance, **sebum**, made in tiny glands (see page 12). Sebum helps to keep the hair soft, but can also attract dirt. Dandruff usually occurs if the hair is extra greasy and washing with a mild shampoo regularly will help control it.

Why does hair go grey?

As we get older, hairs form with microscopic cracks, and these have tiny air bubbles in them. This makes the hairs look grey. Scientists do not know why this happens. A severe shock can make this happen very quickly and a person may appear to have gone grey 'overnight'.

Fascinating facts!

★ The record for the longest hair goes to an old monk in Madras who had hair 8.8 metres long when he died in 1949.

★ There are about 100,000 hairs on your scalp and hundreds of thousands all over your body.

★ Hair is very strong. The average adult could be lifted by a rope made from just 1000 hairs.

Skin

What does the skin do?

Apart from sprouting hairs, the skin has several even more important uses:
1 It forms a barrier, protecting the internal organs from infection.
2 It protects the internal organs from harmful ultra-violet rays from the sun.
3 It is waterproof and holds in the fluid that bathes our cells.
4 It keeps the body temperature even by flushing and sweating.
5 It forms a tough coating that resists wear and tear.
6 It has the sense of touch.

What is skin made of?

*The skin has two main layers. The tough outer layer is called the **epidermis** and is made up of a sheet of flattened cells that are either dead or dying. They are constantly being worn away – every time you dry yourself with a towel you lose some of your dead outer skin cells. Luckily they are being replaced just as quickly from inside. The inner layer is called the **dermis**. This contains the hair follicles, sebaceous glands, sweat glands, nerve endings and blood vessels. The little blood vessels close to the surface of the dermis give skin its pink colour. If you are black or brown, the amount of pigment in your skin will stop the red blood vessels showing through.*

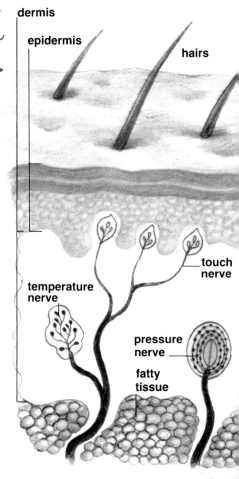

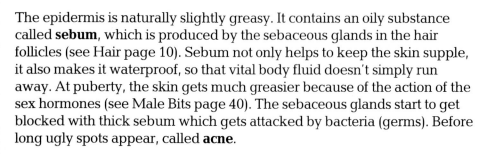

How does skin feel?

Scattered throughout the dermis are millions of nerve endings which can detect pain, touch, heat, cold and pressure. The most sensitive part of the body as far as touch is concerned is the lips; the least sensitive part is the small of the back. The most sensitive part for pressure is the fingers, and the least sensitive is the bottom. This last point is rather important, otherwise sitting down would be agony!

What makes skin greasy?

The epidermis is naturally slightly greasy. It contains an oily substance called **sebum**, which is produced by the sebaceous glands in the hair follicles (see Hair page 10). Sebum not only helps to keep the skin supple, it also makes it waterproof, so that vital body fluid doesn't simply run away. At puberty, the skin gets much greasier because of the action of the sex hormones (see Male Bits page 40). The sebaceous glands start to get blocked with thick sebum which gets attacked by bacteria (germs). Before long ugly spots appear, called **acne**.

What are freckles, moles, birthmarks and warts?

Freckles are tiny patches of skin containing extra pigment.
Birthmarks are usually patches of skin with either an extra large number of tiny blood vessels or more than usual amount of pigment.
Moles are small areas with more than the usual amount of pigment.
Warts are small harmless growths on the skin caused by a certain germ. They sometimes vanish overnight as if by magic, but usually have to be removed by a doctor, if they bother you.

Why do people have different colour skins?

The colour of your skin depends on how much of a pigment called **melanin** (see Hair page 10) there is in the epidermis. Black people's skin has a lot of melanin; white people's very little (except when they have been in the sun). After about three days in the sun, the skin reacts by producing lots of melanin, and a suntan appears. The melanin protects the skin from harmful ultra-voilet rays and helps to avoid painful sunburn.

Why do we sweat?

To keep cool. Dip one hand in some warm water and shake off most of it. Now, hold both hands in front of your face, and blow first on the dry hand and then on the wet one. The wet hand feels cooler, even though the water was warmer. This is because the water, when it dries in the air, causes cooling of the skin.

What is sweat?

Next time you get sweaty, taste a drop. The reason why it tastes salty is that it contains a mixture of liquid and sodium chloride, the same stuff as salt. It is produced in tiny coiled tubes in the dermis, called sweat glands.

How does skin heal?

When you cut yourself, you bleed. While you're deciding whether or not to cry, the blood in the cut is beginning to form a jelly-like mass, a **clot**. This stops further bleeding. For exactly what happens see Blood page 29. When the scab is formed, special cells under it, called **fibroblasts**, move into the wound and start to repair it with a fibrous tissue called **scar tissue**. Next, new skin cells spread across the wound from either side under the scab, and when the skin is healed the scab drops off.

Experiment:

Get 2 sharp pencils and hold them side by side so that the points are pricking your cheek. Gradually move the pencils apart and note when you can feel two definite separate points. Now do the same thing on your lips. You will find you can feel the two points separately only a tiny distance apart, proving how sensitive lips are.

Fascinating Facts

★ The skin has about 3 million sweat glands, and if they were stretched out and laid end to end, they would reach a length of 48 km.

★ The average person sweats about 0.3 litres a day, but in hot, humid conditions, you can lose up to 2.2 litres.

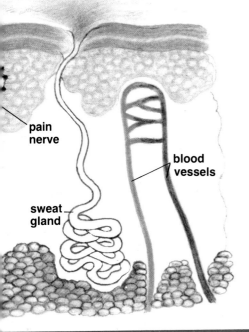

pain nerve

blood vessels

sweat gland

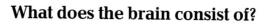

Brain

What does the brain consist of?

The average adult man's brain weighs about 1.3 kg and looks and feels like pink blancmange. It contains 14,000 million nerve cells called **neurones**. Because each neurone is connected to several others, there are zillions of possible combinations, which is why the human brain is so complex and powerful. The average woman's brain is slightly smaller than the man's, but has exactly the same intelligence and memory.

*The thinking part of the brain is the outer layer called the **cortex**, which has a wrinkled and grooved appearance. The deepest groove divides the brain into two halves, the **left** and **right hemispheres**. If a cross-section of the brain is looked at under a microscope, you can see that the cortex consists mostly of what is called 'grey matter' or in fact neurones, while the inner core of the brain is mostly 'white matter' or nerve fibres.*

*The other important parts of the brain are the **cerebellum** which controls the muscles and balance, and the **brain stem** which controls 'automatic' functions over which we have no control, like breathing and heartbeat.*

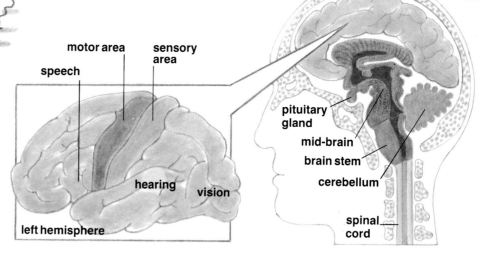

What does the brain do?

Your brain is more skilful in its thinking and more creative in its imagination than any computer anywhere. Yes, even *your* brain! As well as acting as a computer, your brain is also a mixture of telephone exchange, control centre, memory bank, switching station and word processor. It fits snugly in the upper rounded part of the skull called the **cranium**. The brain is covered with a layer of blood vessels and is bathed in protective fluid.

The brain sends and receives messages to and from organs and tissues all over the body, via the **nerves**. These act like telephone wires, running throughout the body, connecting organs and tissues with the spinal cord and brain. For more about this see Body Systems on page 6.

What happens when the brain receives a signal?

When signals have travelled up the nerve fibres in the spinal cord to the brain, they pass through the 'white matter' to a special part of the cortex – the **sensory** area. This interprets the messages and then 'informs' the rest of the cortex. The information is considered and if the cortex decides to do something about it, it orders another special part – the **motor** area – to organise the necessary action. Messages then pass down from the motor area, through the white matter, down the spinal cord and along the nerves to the muscles.

Messages from the sense organs in the skull (eyes, ears, nose and tongue) pass directly from the sense organ, along nerves connected to the inner core of the brain. From here they pass through the white matter to a special area of the cortex which deals with each particular sense.

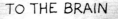

TO THE BRAIN

The two halves of the brain

How do the nerve cells or neurones work?

There are three types of nerve cell:

1 Motor nerve cell which carries messages from the brain to a muscle.

2 Sensory nerve cell which sends messages from sense cells to the brain.

3 Relay nerve cell which relays messages from one part of the brain or spinal cord to another.

*The structure of these cells is basically the same. They are made up of a **cell body** which controls the activities of the cell and an **axon**, or long fibre, leading from the cell body, with branches at its end. The axon relays the message to the next nerve cell. The message is picked up by small branches called **dendrites** which pass it on through their cell body to the next axon.*

nerve cell

dendrite

axon

synapse

*There are tiny gaps, called **synapses** between the ends of the axon and the dendrites of the next nerve cell. The messages jump across the gap from the terminal (end) to the dendrite.*

For what happens in the spinal cord see Back, page 34.

Why does the brain have two halves?

The right and left hemispheres of the brain seem to have different functions. The left side specializes in logical thinking – step-by-step reasoning – calculating, speaking and writing. The right hemisphere is more artistic and creative and more emotional. They do work together as a team, but most of us are influenced by one side more than the other, either more artistic or better at things like maths.

Why do we need sleep?

We spend about a third of our lives asleep! It sounds a terrible waste of time, but it's necessary for the brain to relax and recover from the day's mental exercise. Even during sleep however the brain is not completely at rest. On average you dream five or six times a night, although you probably only remember the last dream.

nerve to muscle

nerve ending

Fascinating Facts

★ Electrical signals travel along nerves at speeds up to 400 km per hour.

★ Your brain is 80% water. The average adult has about 75 km of nerves throughout the body.

Quiz
Match the words with the clues:
a) Synapse   i) Boney dome
b) Neurone   ii) Nerve cell
c) Cranium   iii) Message gap

Eyes

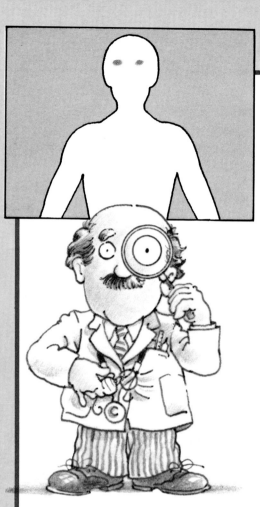

What are eyes made of?

*They are two jelly-filled balls with a hole at the front, (the **pupil**), which lets in light rays. These are focused by a **lens** onto a layer of light-sensitive cells on the **retina**. The coloured ring, the **iris**, makes the pupil bigger or smaller, to adjust the light entering the eye. The **cornea** and **conjunctiva** are two transparent layers which cover the front of the eyeball.*

Why are eyes different colours?

Eyes can be brown, blue, green, grey or some colour in between, depending on the amount of pigment (see Hair page 10) in the round coloured part, the **iris**. The word 'iris' is Greek for 'rainbow'. Pigment in the eyes tends to go with pigment in the hair, so that blue eyes (less pigment) tend to go with fair hair, and brown eyes (more pigment) tend to go with dark hair.

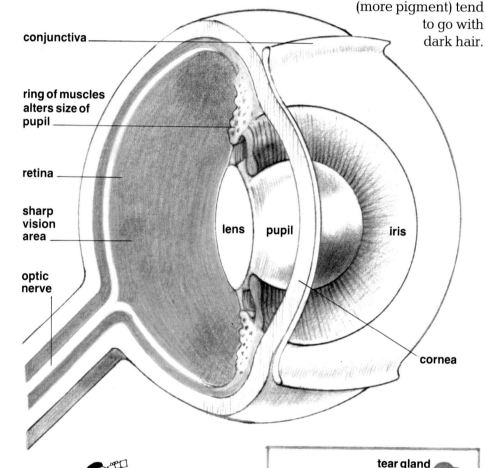

conjunctiva

ring of muscles alters size of pupil

retina

sharp vision area

optic nerve

lens   pupil   iris

cornea

Why do we blink?

Your eyes are the most sensitive and delicate parts of the body. The surface of the eye must be kept moist and clean at all times. Soothing, cleansing fluid is being produced all the time in a special gland in the eye-socket, just above the eyeball. This is the fluid that tears are made of. The purpose of blinking every few seconds is to help spread the tear fluid over the front surface to bathe it. Blinking can also be triggered off by something touching the sensitive eyelashes.

What are tears for?

If the air is smoky or dusty, or if you are standing in a cold wind or peeling onions, your eyes start to water. This is because the amount of tear fluid is greatly increased, to wash away the irritation. Usually tear fluid disappears down a tiny drain-hole in the inner corner of the eye, which leads to the cavity in the nose. When the eye waters, the drain cannot cope with all the fluid, and it wells up, eventually forming tear-drops.

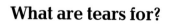

tear gland

tear duct

to nose

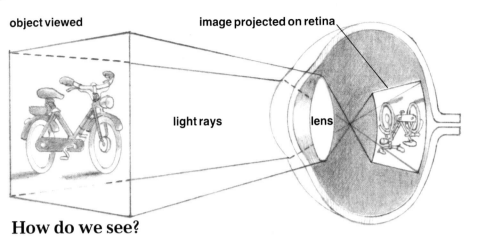

object viewed | image projected on retina | light rays | lens

How do we see?

*The pupil of your eye is like a window, letting in light from the outside world. It looks black, in the same way that the window of a house looks black from the outside. Behind the pupil is a lens which focuses the light so that the rays meet at a point on a 'screen' or retina at the back of the eyeball creating an image. The special cells in the retina fire off a signal when light shines on them. Thousands of tiny nerve fibres collect the signals. These fibres are all brought together at the back of the eyeball, forming the **optic nerve**, which passes through the eyesocket to the brain. In the brain the stream of signals from each optic nerve is constantly being sorted out to re-create the image seen by each eye. The brain blends these two images together to make a single wide picture.*

What are eyelashes for?

They help to keep dust and dirt out of the eyes. If touched they make you blink.

Why do some people need glasses?

We all have different shaped faces. It's not surprising then that our eyeballs also vary in shape. Instead of being perfectly round, some people's eyeballs are slightly egg-shaped. If an eyeball is a bit too long from front to back, the light rays from distant objects cannot focus exactly on the retina. The eye can only see things clearly close to and is 'short sighted'. It is the opposite for 'long sight'. Vision can be made better by wearing an extra lens in front of the eye to alter the focus of the rays.

Short and long sight

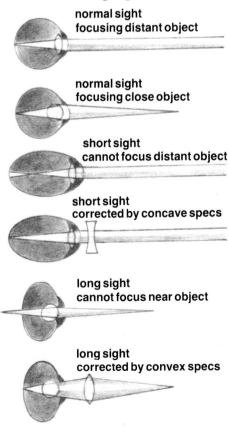

normal sight
focusing distant object

normal sight
focusing close object

short sight
cannot focus distant object

short sight
corrected by concave specs

long sight
cannot focus near object

long sight
corrected by convex specs

Why do we have two eyes?

Having two eyes allows us to see in '3-D' or three dimensions, so that we can judge distance and depth. This was very important to our ape ancestors who had to swing from tree to tree. It would have been very embarrassing if they had kept on missing! Your eyes are about 6.2 cm apart, which means that they see objects from a slightly different point of view. The brain fits these two images together to give the impression of depth. This is called **stereoscopic vision**.

How does the eye see colours?

The light-sensitive cells in the retina consist of 125 million cells called **rods** and 7 million called **cones**. The rods can detect the brightness of the light shining on them. The cones can detect its colour. There are three types of cones, each sensitive to one of the three 'primary colours', red, blue and green.

Fascinating Facts

★ The human eye is so sensitive that a person sitting on a hilltop, on a clear moonless night, could see a match being struck up to 80 km away!

Experiment

Watch your eyes in a mirror, and see how often you blink. The average is about six times a minute. Do a sum and add up all your blinks during an average day. You'll be surprised how long you spend with your eyes shut.

Ears

Why is the human ear such a strange shape?

Most mammals have large ears which stand away from their heads and which can swivel to point towards sounds. This helps them to find out where danger might be coming from. Humans, with few enemies, have less need for such sensitive hearing and so our ears are smaller, flatter and less mobile. (That goes for most of us anyway!) Small flat ears are best for hearing all sorts of sounds from lots of different directions at once. We do have some muscles for moving our ears and some people can waggle them quite noticeably! The ridges in the ear help it to spring back to the right shape if it gets bent.

Where does the ear hole go?

The ear is made up of three different parts: the outer ear consists of the **pinna** *and* **ear canal** *and leads to the* **ear-drum**, *a thin and delicate membrane stretched across the canal like a drum-skin. The middle ear has the three small bones – the* **anvil**, **hammer** *and* **stirrup** *and the* **Eustachian tube** *which goes to the back of the throat and controls the air pressure. The inner ear contains the* **cochlea** *and the* **semi-circular canals**.

How do ears hear?

Sound consists of vibrations reaching the ear where they are changed into signals which are carried to the brain. The brain interprets the signals as the feeling that we call sound.

The sound waves make the ear-drum vibrate. It in turn makes the three tiny bones vibrate. The stirrup acts like a piston vibrating the fluid in the cochlea. As this fluid moves, it excites special cells which send signals to the brain along the **auditory nerve.**

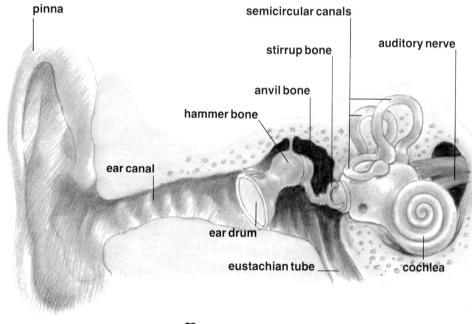

pinna · ear canal · ear drum · eustachian tube · hammer bone · anvil bone · stirrup bone · semicircular canals · auditory nerve · cochlea

How can the ear tell high notes from low ones?

The difference between high notes and low notes depends on how quickly the sound waves are vibrating. Low notes vibrate slowly and high notes quickly. The cochlea, where the vibrations are sorted out, is a snail-like spiral which is actually a tube inside a tube. Uncurled, it is 3.5 cm long. The inner tube runs the whole length and consists of an incredibly thin membrane resting on a row of special cells which are sensitive to vibration. High notes shake one part of the membrane, low notes another. The special cells tell which part of the membrane is being vibrated and the brain interprets the signals as different notes.

Why do we have two ears?

By having an ear on each side of our heads we can tell which direction a sound is coming from. By comparing the sound waves reaching each ear, the brain is able to work out the position of the sound.

What makes people deaf?

Too much loud noise can damage the cells in the cochlea. Some people are born deaf. Some suffer from infections of the middle ear. In some older people the piston gets stuck, and for some deafness is caused by the special cells failing to send signals to the brain. This is called 'nerve deafness'.

How do ears help us balance?

There is a part of the inner ear which has nothing to do with hearing. Its job is to tell us what position our head is in and which way it is being moved. The balance-and-movement detector consists of three semi-circular tubes or canals set at right angles to each other. They contain a fluid and special cells to detect how the fluid is moving in the cell. When you turn your head one of the canals moves but the fluid stays still.

Experiment

Sprinkle some pepper on to some water in a glass and twist the glass. The water will stay still but the glass moves. This happens in the canals in your ear.

Why are ears waxy?

Dirt and dust can get into the ear-hole. The skin lining the ear hole produces a soft waxy material which slowly works its way out, taking any dirt and dust with it. If the wax gets too hard it can block the ear and cause slight deafness and irritation, in which case the doctor may have to remove the plug by syringing your ear.

How can we tell if we are upside down or not?

Your position detector is next to the semi-circular canals. It is a tiny bundle of bone-like granules attached to a pad of pressure-sensitive cells. Your position affects the pressure of the granules on the cells and the brain can work out whether you are lying or standing or upside down.

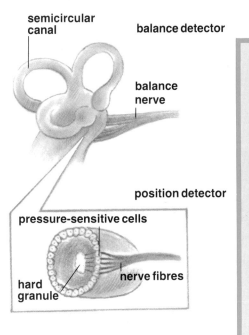

semicircular canal

balance detector

balance nerve

position detector

pressure-sensitive cells

hard granule

nerve fibres

Fascinating facts

★ The lowest note a human ear can hear is a low rumble vibrating at 20 times a second. The highest note is a very high hiss, vibrating at 20,000 times a second.

★ The loudness of sound is measured in units called **decibels** (dB). The softest sound we can hear is about 10dB, a ticking watch 20dB, normal conversation 60dB, a rock concert 100dB and a pneumatic drill 120dB. Sounds above 90dB can cause pain, and possibly deafness.

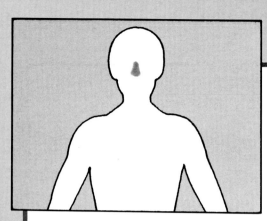

Nose

Where do the nostrils go to?

Each nostril leads back into a cavity, and the air swirls about, passes back over the roof of the mouth, then whizzes down your throat and into your windpipe.

Why are nostrils hairy?

To trap dust and dirt which would irritate your lungs.

Why do we sniff to smell things?

Sniffing makes things easier to smell. Usually when you are breathing normally through your nose the air passes straight back to your throat, and very little wafts up to the receptor cells in the roof of the nasal cavity. But by sniffing hard and long, you can direct the airstream straight at the sensitive smell organ.

How does the nose smell?

*The smell detectors consist of a patch of special cells (or **olfactory receptors**) covered with tiny hairs and a sticky jelly which absorbs smelly molecules from the air. The cells send coded signals to the brain along the **olfactory nerve**. The brain decodes the signals and notices a smell.*

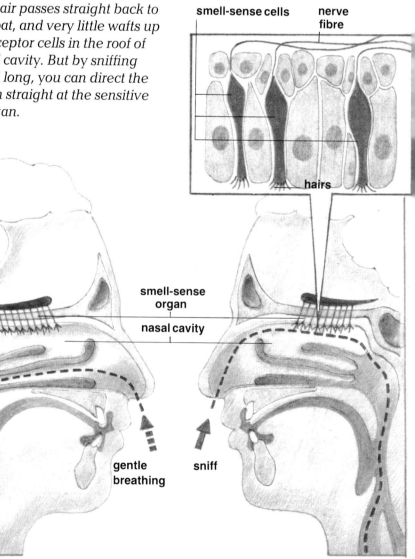

smell-sense cells

nerve fibre

hairs

smell-sense organ

nasal cavity

gentle breathing

sniff

What is the nose for?

As well as getting oxygen into your lungs (see Breathing page 26), your nose is your most sensitive organ. It can detect incredibly tiny quantities of 'smelly' substances in the air and tell thousands of different smells apart.

Why only one nose when we have two eyes and two ears?

Actually you do have two noses! Well two nostrils anyway. Inside your nose the stiff wall separating your nostrils goes nearly all the way back to your throat. The two smell detectors or **olfactory organs** are small patches in the ceiling of each nasal cavity.

But why do different smells smell different?

The human nose can smell a huge number of different scents. It is said that the best perfume makers can tell apart over 10,000 odours! Nobody knows how the nose does it. One theory is that there are seven basic smells and that the others are all a combination of these. The smelly seven are floral, pepperminty, musky, ethereal, mothbally, pungent and putrid. This means that there are seven different types of receptor cell, each one only reacting to one of the basic smells. If a smelly substance has some of that primary smell it will trigger off that particular type of cell, in the same way that a key will fit only one particular type of lock. The brain gets signals from a combination of these cells and interprets the pattern of signals as sausages frying, or whatever. A dog's nose is a million times more sensitive than a human's. This is partly because the dog's smell organ is much longer and larger than ours.

Why does having a cold spoil our sense of smell?

When you have a cold, your nasal membranes defend themselves against the virus by producing large amounts of mucus which becomes thick and yellowish. Yuk! All this gunge blocks the nose and stops air reaching the smell organ.

Yes, but why does it spoil the sense of taste?

Because your sense of taste depends a great deal on your sense of smell. The taste buds can taste only a few basic tastes (see Mouth page 22). What gives food its flavour is the fact that smells from the food reach the nose during eating. Without your nose, food tastes pretty boring.

Why do we sneeze?

Sneezing is one of those automatic or 'reflex' actions which we cannot really control. Its purpose is to blow out the dust or whatever is in the nose causing an irritation. In a sneeze the air is forced out through the nose at very high speeds of over 160km per hour! In normal breathing the air travels at a mere 8kph. When we feel a sneeze coming we take a sharp breath in, we close our mouth and our soft palate, and we suddenly force a breath out. This builds up a high pressure of air. The sneeze is the sudden release of this pressure through the nose. Atchoo!

What are adenoids and sinuses?

Adenoids are fleshy pads at the back of the nose above the soft palate. Like tonsils (see Throat page 24) they fight infection and can become swollen. Sinuses are the air-filled nasal cavities in the bones of the face, which connect with the nostrils and windpipe. With a bad cold the sinuses can become blocked with mucus or inflamed.

Fascinating facts

★ About 250,000,000,000 bits of the smelly substance in sweat are left in a footprint. This is how dogs can follow a person's trail by scent.

Experiment:

Cut an apple and a potato into pieces of roughly the same size and shape. Now get someone to blindfold you and put one of the pieces into your mouth while holding your nose. You will find it very difficult to tell whether you're tasting the apple or the potato.

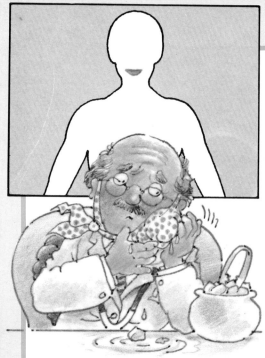

Mouth

Why are lips red?

Put the tip of your tongue on the skin above your upper lip then move it down onto your lip. Notice how much smoother your lip feels. This is because your skin here is much thinner than the outer layer of ordinary skin. It is so see-through that the tiny blood vessels show through. It is the redness of the blood in the tiny vessels that makes lips look red.

How do lips make words?

Our soft fleshy lips have strong muscles which means that they can move about a lot. When the lips are forced open by you blowing air out, they make a 'b' or a 'p' sound. And by altering their shape they can make vowels like 'eee' and 'ooo'. To show how important the lips are in making sounds, pretend that you are a ventriloquist and try to say, 'My very best pal Bobby' without moving your lips! Usually your tongue does most of the talking. You won't have any trouble saying, 'It's a grand day to go to the seaside isn't it?', without moving your lips, because here the tongue is doing all the work.

What are teeth made of?

Mainly a bone-like stuff called **dentine**, *which is like the ivory of an elephant's tusk. The dentine is protected by a very hard layer of* **enamel** *and at the centre of the tooth is a soft core or* **pulp**, *with blood vessels and a nerve ending. The root of the tooth is fixed to the tooth-socket in the jaw-bone by a layer of so-called* **cement**.

Why are teeth such different shapes?

Because they all do different jobs in eating. The front teeth, or **incisors**, *act like scissors cutting or shearing the food. Then there are the* **canines**, *which are a bit like fangs. Their job is to grip and tear food, especially meat, which is why they are so sharp in meat-eating animals like lions and wolves. Then further back are the* **pre-molars** *and* **molars** *which are for chewing and grinding, especially vegetable matter. This is why molars are the main type of teeth in grass- and leaf-eating animals like rabbits and cows. As your jaws grow bigger, you lose your first set of teeth ('baby' or 'milk' teeth) and grow a bigger set of permanent teeth, 32 in all. Each side of each jaw has two incisors, one canine, two pre-molars and three molars.*

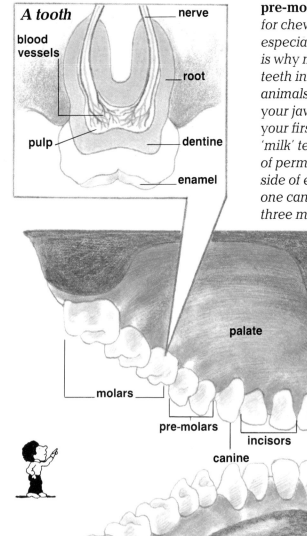

A *tooth* — nerve, blood vessels, root, pulp, dentine, enamel

palate, molars, pre-molars, incisors, canine, tongue

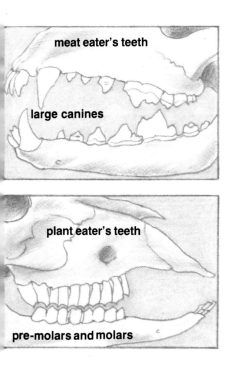

meat eater's teeth

large canines

plant eater's teeth

pre-molars and molars

How does the tongue taste things?

*The tongue is covered with about 3000 taste-buds. These are tiny pits in the surface lined with special taste-sensitive cells. There are four basic types of taste called **primary taste sensations**. These are salty, sweet, bitter and sour. Some taste-buds are better at one particular taste than others. Taste-buds at the tip of the tongue are good at salty things. A bit further back on each side are most of the buds for sweet things. Further back still are the sour taste-buds. Right at the back of the tongue and also over the soft palate and sides of the throat are the bitter-tasting buds. The effect of the bitter buds lasts longer which is why you may often have a bitter taste in your mouth some time after eating. Signals from the taste-buds pass along nerves to the taste-centre, near the smell-centre in the brain. Here the signals are interpreted as the combination of tastes we know so well.*

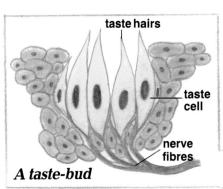

taste hairs

taste cell

nerve fibres

A taste-bud

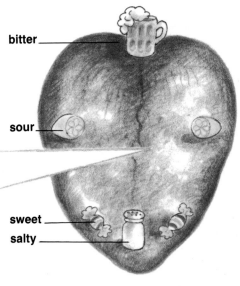

bitter

sour

sweet

salty

Why is toothbrushing important?

Because, although the enamel that coats your teeth is the hardest stuff in the whole body, it is easily dissolved by acid. Unfortunately, whenever you eat, you leave tiny amounts of food in the spaces around your teeth. Bacteria (germs) in the mouth live on this and produce a sticky layer over the teeth called **plaque**. Sugary substances are turned to acid by the plaque and the acid then attacks the enamel causing holes in your teeth.

What is saliva?

Saliva is the proper name for spit. See how many cream crackers you can eat, without a drink of water, in one minute. I'll bet you can't even manage two! That's because you can't make enough saliva fast enough to soften and wet them ready for swallowing. Without saliva, the food just sticks in your mouth and would probably choke you if you tried to swallow it. Saliva mixes with food in chewing and makes a smooth easy-to-swallow paste. It also contains a chemical called an **enzyme** (see Tummy page 36) which begins to digest the food. Saliva comes from special glands under the tongue and in the cheeks. The taste, smell or even the thought of food makes these glands pour saliva along little pipes or **ducts** into the mouth.

How does the tongue move?

The tongue is really just a muscle, which can curl about in all directions. It plays an important part in speech. It also sorts and positions your food as you chew and swallow (see Throat page 24).

Fascinating Facts

★ How fast can you count out loud? Try counting up to 100. You might just manage it in 30 seconds, but I bet you make lots of mistakes. The fastest talker on the radio was the BBC commentator Raymond Glendenning who once spoke 176 words in 30 seconds while following a greyhound race.

Quiz

Which of the following words use your lips, and which use your tongue:
Dad/Mum/memory/teeth?

Throat

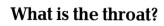

What is the throat?

It is the hollow space behind your mouth which your nasal passages go into, and your windpipe (**trachea**) and food tube (**oesophagus**) lead out of. It also contains your voice-box (**larynx**) and **tonsils**.

What are tonsils for?

They are two fleshy wrinkled pads of tissue on either side of your throat just behind your tongue. You can see them if you look in a mirror, stick out your tongue and say 'aaaaah'! Although you can exist without tonsils, they do help to defend the body against invasion by bacteria (germs).

The tonsils act as a pair of forts guarding the throat. They contain millions of white cell 'soldiers' (see Blood, page 28). These pounce on the invading germs and have a battle with them.

What is the Adam's Apple for?

It's for making sounds. It's the voice-box or **larynx**. *It sits at the top of the windpipe and has a stiff outer casing which acts as a collar round the windpipe, coming to quite a sharp point at the front. That's what bobs up and down when you swallow. Inside there are two stiff membranes stretched across the windpipe side by side – the* **vocal cords**. *Usually they are opened wide apart for quiet breathing. If they are nearly closed they can be made to vibrate by whizzing air past them, producing a note. The stronger you breathe out through the slit between the cords, the louder the sound. The cords can be tightened to make higher notes, or relaxed more to make lower ones.*

The Battle of the Tonsils

What is that floppy thing in the middle of the throat?

It's called the **uvula** but nobody knows what it's for.

Why do boys' voices 'break'?

The length of the vocal cords and the size of the larynx affects how high or low your voice is. Children have small larynxes and high voices. At **puberty** (see page 41) boys' cords grow twice as fast as girls'. This makes boys' voices become suddenly deeper, or 'break'.

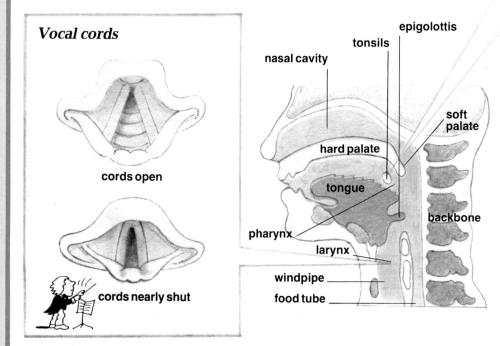

Vocal cords

cords open

cords nearly shut

epigolottis

tonsils

nasal cavity

soft palate

hard palate

tongue

backbone

pharynx

larynx

windpipe

food tube

Why does the Adam's Apple go up and down when you swallow?

This is to stop the food going down the wrong way. At the back of your tongue, just 'down the hatch', is a large flap of tissue called the **epiglottis**. *When you are breathing it just sits there. The air doesn't go down the food tube because it is shut off by the* **larynx**. *But when you swallow, a complicated process occurs which switches the direction of the channel through the throat, rather like the points on a train-set.*

Your larynx rises upwards and then forwards, tucking itself under the epiglottis, which forms a tight seal over the windpipe. At the same time your tongue squeezes up against your hard palate pushing the food or drink up and back, and your soft palate blocks off the nasal passages so that nothing goes up your nose. There's only one way the food can go and that is down the food tube which has been opened up by the movement of the larynx.

A peristaltic wave pushing food down

What happens if food goes down the wrong way?

If by accident some food or drink gets into the larynx, it is immediately detected by cells which are extremely sensitive to touch. They send signals to the brain to make you cough the gate-crashing particles out.

Swallowing

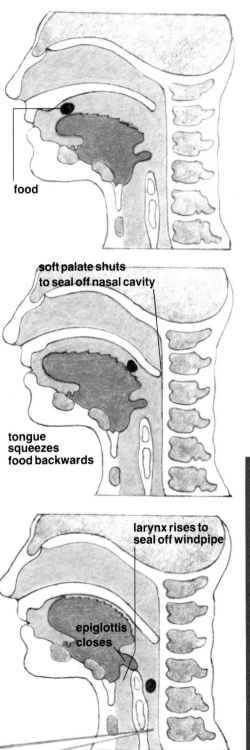

food

soft palate shuts to seal off nasal cavity

tongue squeezes food backwards

larynx rises to seal off windpipe

epiglottis closes

Can you swallow upside-down?

Try it with a glass of water and a bendy straw, stand on your head and take a few sips. It works! Of course it's not that clever, horses and giraffes do it all the time. It works because the food tube is made of thousands of circular bands of muscle fibres, known as **smooth muscle** because their action is smooth and slow, in waves called **peristaltic waves**. The bands tighten one after another from the throat to the stomach, squeezing the food or drink down the food tube rather like squeezing toothpaste down the tube. When the food or drink reaches the stomach a valve opens and shuts to let it in. For the rest of the story of digestion see page 36.

Fascinating Facts

★ Vocal cords grow from about 6 mm at birth to about 30 mm for an adult man. An adult woman's vocal cords are smaller — about 20 mm long.

★ The average adult person can sing about two octaves from highest to lowest notes. The deepest bass voice can reach notes below the lowest on the piano. The highest soprano singers can sing notes higher than the piano.

Breathing

Why do we breathe?

Breathing is something you do all the time, usually without noticing. It's only when you get puffed that you realise how much your body needs air. You can't 'forget' to breathe because it is a fully automatic process. Try holding your breath for a little while (don't overdo it!). Notice how you get a stronger and stronger feeling that you want to take a breath. Eventually you have to give in – which is lucky because otherwise you would suffocate! The control centre in your brain is sending emergency signals to your chest to get gasping again straight away.

Breathing has two vital purposes. Firstly it puts **oxygen** from the air into your body. Secondly it removes waste **carbon dioxide** from your body into the air. Oxygen is needed by every cell in your body. Without it the cells will die within a few minutes. Similarly, every cell makes a waste gas called carbon dioxide which must be got rid of quickly or the cell will die.

How do our lungs work?

*Each of your two lungs is connected to your windpipe (**trachea**) by a tube called the **main bronchus**. Within each lung the bronchus divides into branches like a tree. The very tiniest twigs are microscopic in size and each one ends in a minute bubble called an **alveolus**. There are about 3 million alveoli in your lungs, so that each lung is rather like a large sponge. All these branches and bubbles give the lungs an enormous surface area.*

Every bubble is wrapped in a network of tiny blood vessels called capillaries (see page 31) so that oxygen can pass easily from the air in the bubble to the blood in the capillaries, which then carries it off to the rest of the body. Carbon dioxide passes from the blood to the air in the bubbles to be breathed out.

How much and how fast do we breathe?

Most people take about 12-15 breaths a minute when they are sitting or lying quietly. The air usually passes in and out through the nose at about 8 kmph. The most air that a person can breathe in and out in one breath is about 5 litres. (You need most oxygen when taking strenuous exercise.) But usually the volume of each breath is only about one-tenth of that.

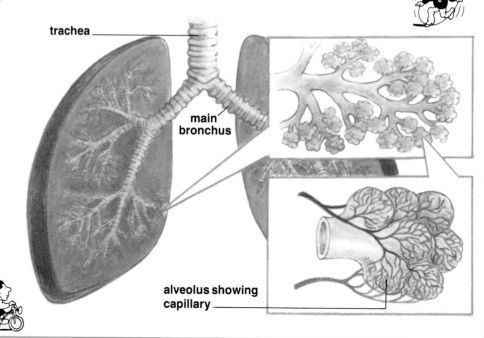

trachea

main bronchus

alveolus showing capillary

How does air get into the lungs?

Getting the air in and out of the lungs is called **respiration**. *It is the work of the chest muscles and the* **diaphragm**, *a thin sheet of muscle which forms an elastic floor to the chest cavity, rather like a trampoline.*

When you take a deep breath, the ribs move outwards and upwards, expanding your ribcage. At the same time your diaphragm moves downwards. Air is sucked into the lungs. As you relax and let your breath go, the ribs and diaphragm spring back into the resting position and push the air out.

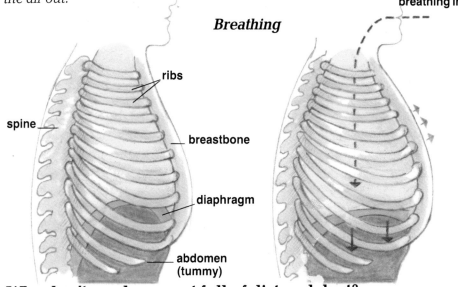

Breathing

breathing in

ribs

spine

breastbone

diaphragm

abdomen
(tummy)

Why don't our lungs get full of dirt and dust?

Lungs have a remarkable self-cleaning system. The inner lining of the air tubes has a layer of special cells. Some of these produce a sticky fluid called mucus which traps the dirt. All the other cells have tiny hairs on them which wave the mucus up from the lungs into the windpipe to be coughed up. The poisons in cigarette smoke paralyse the hair cells and destroy the lung's self-cleaning system, so that dirt collects in the lungs.

What happens when you cough?

A cough is usually an automatic action to get rid of irritating particles from the air tubes and lungs. Your vocal cords (see page 24) close tightly and your respiratory muscles contract, building up pressure. Then suddenly your vocal cords open letting the air out, sometimes at a speed of 100 kph. Coughing can be very difficult to control.

COUGH! COUGH!

What is a hiccup (or hiccough)?

It is a sudden breath in, followed by a sharp closing of the vocal cords – hic! It may be caused by gulping too much air which makes the diaphragm contract.

Why do we yawn?

A primitive reflex action, even newborn babies and animals yawn. There is no simple explanation. One theory is that it tones up the breathing muscles; another that it increases the blood supply to the drowsy or bored brain by making you take in a big breath.

What is laughing?

Again, a reflex form of expression. Newborn babies can smile but do not learn to laugh for several months. Laughter consists of a long breath out punctuated by a series of 'h' sounds. Tickle your ribs and listen. Hahahahahahah!

Fascinating facts

★ If you flattened out all the bubbles in the lungs, they would cover an area the size of a tennis court.

★ The average adult breathes about 15 cubic metres of air a day. That's the amount of air in a small bedroom or 6 telephone boxes.

Quiz
Complete this sentence:
We breathe in _____ and breathe out _____ _____ .

Blood

What is blood for?

To carry substances rapidly from one part of the body to another (see Heart page 30).

1 It carries **oxygen** from the lungs to the cells all over the body.

2 It carries **carbon dioxide**, a waste product that must be removed, to the lungs to be breathed out.

3 It carries vital products like **glucose** from storage in the liver to the tissues.

4 It takes away poisonous waste-products like **urea** from the tissues and carries them to the kidneys for removal in the urine.

5 It distributes **water and minerals** round the body where they are needed.

6 It carries **hormones**, the chemical messengers of the body.

7 It defends the body against infection by ambushing alien bugs with white cell 'soldiers'.

8 It acts as a central heating system, keeping all parts of the body warm.

9 It contains substances which help to plug any leaks that may occur. So all in all it is pretty impressive stuff!

Why is it red?

Blood is a very complicated mixture consisting of about 50% water in which a great many different substances are dissolved and containing a large number of cells. The average adult has 6 litres of it.

Nearly all the cells are red blood cells which contain a red pigment with a lot of iron in it, called **haemoglobin**. This can absorb huge quantities of oxygen and carry it from the lungs to the tissues. When it has just been filled with oxygen, haemoglobin is bright red. When the tissues have used up all the oxygen, the haemoglobin is dark purply-maroon in colour. It is thought that the mixture of oxygen and iron makes the blood red. Shellfish, whose blood has copper in it instead of iron, have green blood!

What else does blood consist of?

Blood, like sweat, tastes salty. The water that the cells float in is a diluted solution of salt and other substances, including some special proteins that help to stop the water soaking away into the tissues. This watery fluid with the cells removed has a yellowish tinge, and is cloudy and sticky. It is called **plasma**. The rest of the blood (about 40%) consists of the blood cells.

*A red blood cell is shaped rather like a doughnut with a membrane over where the hole would be. All red cells are the same and very boring compared to white ones. White blood cells, or **leucocytes**,*

Blood cells as seen through a microscope

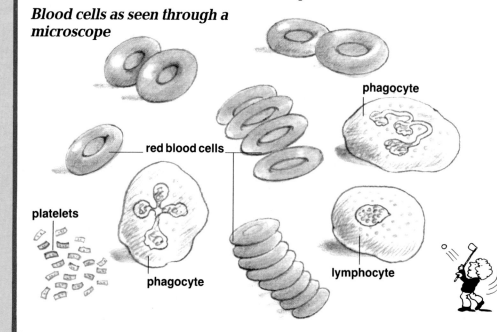

phagocyte

red blood cells

platelets

phagocyte

lymphocyte

*are larger than their red cousins and are of two main types. Two-thirds of them (**phagocytes**) do their job of fighting infection by actually gobbling up the germs. The other third, **lymphocytes**, work either by attaching themselves to invading viruses and dissolving them to bits or by making poisons called **antibodies**, each designed to kill a particular type of germ. Platelets are tiny particles, much smaller than blood cells which help to form blood clots and plug leaks in the circulation.*

What is a blood group?

Not all blood is the same. We each have a slightly different type of blood. This can only be shown by special laboratory tests, called blood-typing or blood-grouping, and four main groups have been discovered. There are two types of test:

1 The A-B-O test which tells whether your blood is Group A, B, AB or O.
2 The Rhesus test which will show that you are either Rh-positive or Rh-negative. When someone has a blood transfusion, they must be given the right blood group.

Where does blood come from?

Your blood is constantly being made and replaced. The red cells and platelets are made in the soft tissue in the hollow centres of your bones, called the **bone marrow**. The white cells are partly made in the bone marrow but mostly in special clumps of tissue called **lymph nodes** (see Body Systems page 7).

How does blood clot?

*Blood clotting is started by the tiny platelets floating amongst the blood cells. These are the emergency plumbers of the circulation. Within minutes of detecting damage, they become sticky and attach themselves to the vessel wall in huge numbers forming a plug. This may be enough to stop the bleeding, but if the wound is large, a blood clot may have to be formed by the platelets releasing substances which trigger chemical reactions in the blood. This forms a mesh of microscopic threads called **fibrin** which traps blood cells in a jelly-like mass. After about half an hour this hardens and forms a scab.*

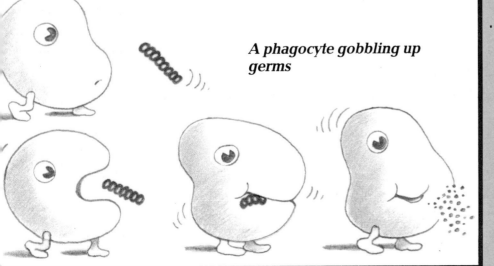

A phagocyte gobbling up germs

Blood clotting

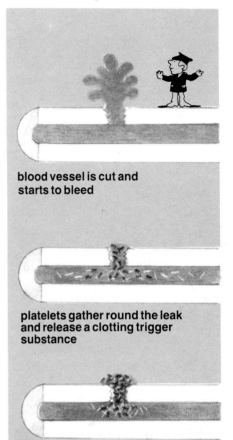

blood vessel is cut and starts to bleed

platelets gather round the leak and release a clotting trigger substance

microscopic threads form which trap blood cells forming a clot to stop bleeding

Fascinating Facts

★ A tiny pin-prick of blood (1 cubic mm) contains about 5 million red blood cells, 5000-10,000 white blood cells and 250,000 platelets.

★ Before each red cell dies (after about 4 months), it will have made about 172,000 journeys around the circulation.

★ About 10,000,000 red cells are destroyed every second, but luckily are replaced just as quickly.

Heart

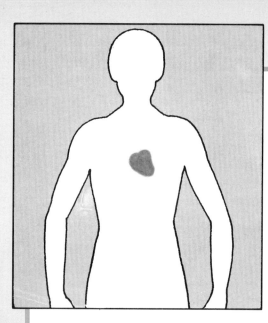

Where is the heart exactly?

Higher up in your chest than you think. It is in the middle of your chest, not on the left side as lots of people think. It feels as though it's on the left because that side of the heart beats much harder than the right side.

What is the heart made of?

A very special kind of muscle, so that it can beat automatically without having to be told to do so by the brain. It is like a bag or pouch of this muscle which twitches every split-second. Inside, the bag is divided into two separate halves by a thick leathery wall. The two halves are called the left side and the right side, and each has a different job to do. The left side pumps blood from the lungs to the rest of the body. The right side pumps blood from the body back to the lungs again.

How does the heart work?

*The heart is like a pump. When the muscle contracts or shortens (see Hands and Arms page 32) blood is squirted out of each side separately. There are drain pipes leading into each side (**veins**) and supply pipes (**arteries**) leading out. The blood always travels in the same direction because there are **valves** to stop it going the wrong way. These are leathery flaps which pop open to let the blood go forwards, but slam shut to stop it leaking backwards. All this popping and slamming makes quite a lot of noise, which the doctor can hear using a stethoscope on the front of your chest. It sounds a bit like 'lub-dup, lub-dup, lub-dup'.*

*The two sides of the heart are each divided into an upper and lower half, making four chambers in all. The two upper ones or **auricles** collect the blood draining from the veins into the heart. Then with each heart-beat the blood is squirted into the lower chambers or **ventricles**. The ventricles are powerful pumps which force the blood into the supply pipes or arteries.*

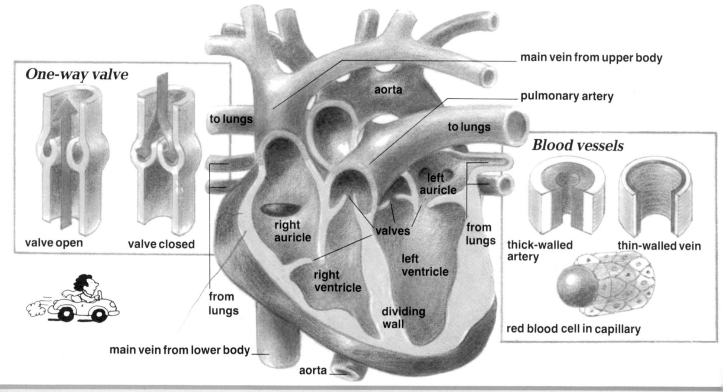

One-way valve

valve open   valve closed

main vein from upper body

aorta

pulmonary artery

to lungs

to lungs

left auricle

Blood vessels

right auricle

valves

from lungs

right ventricle

left ventricle

from lungs

thick-walled artery   thin-walled vein

dividing wall

red blood cell in capillary

main vein from lower body

aorta

Where do the arteries go to?

The arteries carry blood to different parts of the body. The main artery from the right side of the heart (the **pulmonary artery**), takes blood to the lungs to collect oxygen (see Breathing page 26). The main artery from the left side (the **aorta**) branches into lots of smaller arteries taking blood to all the different parts of the body.

What happens to the blood at the end of an artery?

Just like a tree, the arteries branch into smaller and smaller 'twigs'. The tiniest twigs form a network of microscopic channels which thread their way between all the cells. These are called **capillaries** and some are so fine that even the blood cells have to go in single file!

What happens in the capillaries?

This is where the 'goods' are loaded and unloaded. Oxygen passes from the red blood cells through the thin capillary walls into surrounding tissue cells. Carbon dioxide and other waste products pass from the tissue cells into the blood. In the lungs, capillaries collect oxygen and unload carbon dioxide.

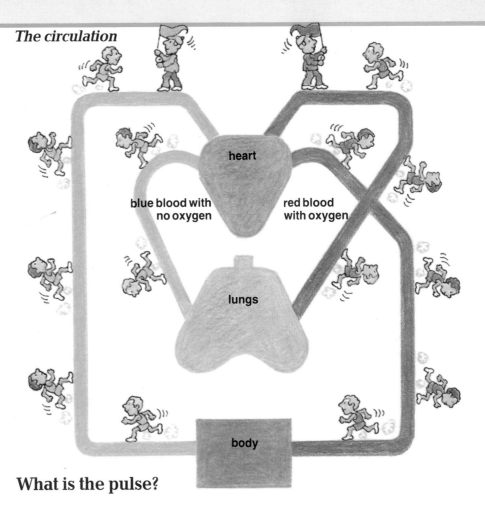

The circulation

heart

blue blood with no oxygen

red blood with oxygen

lungs

body

What is the pulse?

It's a pressure wave that passes along the arteries after every heart beat. It's like when you throw a stone into the middle of a pond and a ripple spreads outwards right to the edges. So each time your heart beats, a ripple or pressure wave spreads outwards from the heart along all the arteries, pushing the blood through.

How fast does the heart beat?

It depends on your age. A baby's heart beats at about 120 per minute but this slows down in an adult to 70-90 per minute.

Where does the blood go after the capillaries?

At the end of a capillary the pressure waves are so weak that the blood no longer flows but oozes. It seeps into thin-walled drainage tubes called **venules**. These join up to form larger tubes called **veins**. The blood in the veins no longer has oxygen in it and is dark purplish coloured. When seen through the skin the veins look blue. The veins get bigger and bigger as the blood drains back to the right side of the heart and the whole process begins again.

Fascinating Facts

★ Your heart is about the size of your clenched fist.

★ An average man has 5-6 litres of blood, the average woman has 4-5 litres.

★ If the heart was lifting us into the air instead of pumping blood around, it would have enough energy to lift us over 300 metres into the sky every day.

★ Elephants' hearts beat at only 25 per minute, while a mouse's heart beats at 600 per minute!

31

Hands and Arms

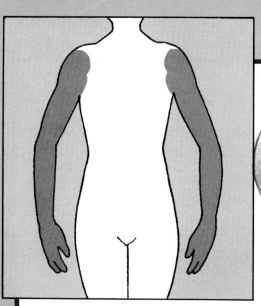

Why do we have four fingers and a thumb?

Lots of mammals have five digits on their 'hands'. Even animals with hooves, like cows and horses, have tiny digits on either side of the greatly enlarged weight-carrying toes. But the big difference in humans is that they have what is called an 'opposing' thumb; in other words one digit that can swing round and work in the opposite direction to the other four. It is this action of the thumb against the fingers that helps our hands to grip things of all shapes and sizes from a pin to a pumpkin.

Why is the hand so handy?

Take a look at your own hand, palm facing you. It consists of a square (the palm) with five flexible clamps attached to it (the fingers and thumb). The four finger clamps are fixed in a row along the far edge of the square and work in one direction only, by curling on themselves or grasping against the palm. The fifth clamp (the thumb) is attached to one of the near corners of the square. It acts as a sort of prop that the fingers can work against, a sturdy buffer.

What do muscles do?

Muscles are what make you move. They are fleshy bundles of tissue which can shorten their length and pull things. Anchored to the two bones on either side of a joint, they can move it. Each muscle is made up of thousands of muscle fibres. On a signal from the brain, a tiny electric current is applied to the fibre and it twitches. If there are enough electrical signals reaching the muscle fibres, the muscle will shorten, or contract. Signals to the muscles travel along nerves from the spinal cord to special relay stations embedded in the sides of the muscle fibres (see Back page 34). Muscles produce movement by pulling on a nearby bone. They can only pull, not push. All the most powerful movements of the hand are made by forearm muscles pulling on very strong cable-like structures called **tendons** *which join the muscles to the hand bones.*

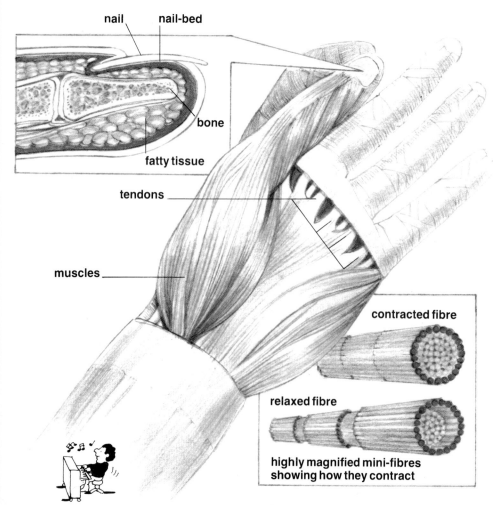

nail   nail-bed

bone

fatty tissue

tendons

muscles

contracted fibre

relaxed fibre

highly magnified mini-fibres showing how they contract

How do joints work?

A joint is the moveable bit between two bones. Where they connect, the bones are coated with a tough layer of tissue called **cartilage**. The bones are held together by very strong straps of tissue called **ligaments**, which stop the joint from being overstretched. There are two main types of joint – **hinge joints** and **ball-and-socket** joints. Hinge joints can only move to and fro in one direction (like a finger joint). But a ball-and-socket joint can move about in all directions, like the shoulder or hip joints.

A hinge joint only needs two muscles to work it, pulling in opposite directions. For example, the elbow is bent by the muscle at the front of the upper arm, the **biceps**. When the biceps contracts, it pulls the forearm upwards. The elbow is straightened by a muscle at the back of the upper arm, the **triceps**. Ball-and-socket joints need four or more muscles to pull the moveable bone in any direction.

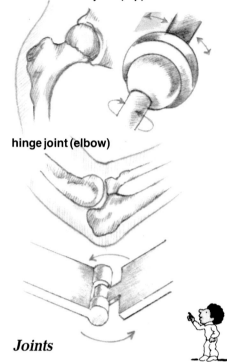

ball and socket joint (hip)

hinge joint (elbow)

Joints

What are nails made of?

Believe it or not, the same stuff as hair – **keratin** (see Hair page 10). Like hair, nails are dead, and they grow in a similar way to hair, by being pushed out of a pit in the skin. The pit, or nail-bed, lies horizontal to the skin and as the nail grows it slides along the surface of the nail-bed to the finger-tip.

Why are most people right-handed?

Nobody really knows. About 19 out of every 20 people are right-handed. The reason is probably due to the way the two halves of the brain work (see Brain page 14). The left side of the brain (the one concerned with speech, maths, thinking etc.) controls the right side of the body and so the right hand is closer to the bit that is best at working out things.

What are fingerprints?

The skin on the palm side of our hands is covered with tiny ridges which act like ridges on car tyres and help you to grip. It just so happens that everyone has slightly different fingerprints and so detectives can identify a crook by taking a 'print' of his finger.

Why are palms so sweaty?

Slight dampness of the palms and fingers helps you to grip smooth things more easily. There are thousands of extra sweat glands to keep the skin soft, supple and clingy (see Skin page 12). The trouble is that if your palms get *too* sweaty, they become slippery. If you have this trouble, you should never get a job as a milkman!

Muscles bending an arm

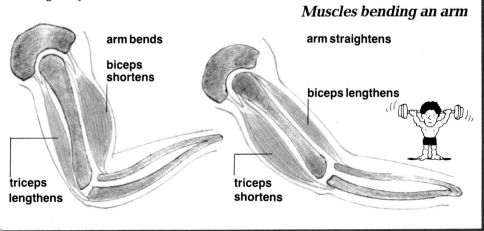

arm bends
biceps shortens
triceps lengthens

arm straightens
biceps lengthens
triceps shortens

Fascinating Facts

★ You have over 650 muscles in your body, making between 30 and 50% of your total weight.

★ The nails of the right hand grow faster than the left in right-handed people and vice versa. The middle fingernail is the fastest of all.

★ The world record for the longest fingernail is 67 cm held by Romesh Sharma of India. It took him 13 years to grow.

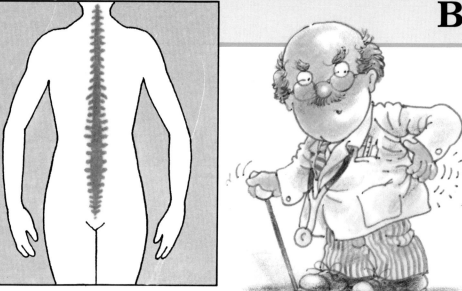

Back

What are those bumps down the spine?

All the vertebrae have a spike of bone sticking out backwards and those are the bumps that you can feel down your back. The spikes act as anchors for the very strong muscles, tendons and ligaments (see Hands and Arms page 32) that support and move your spine. There are similar spikes sticking out sideways which you cannot feel. In the chest part of your back, these sideways spikes also support your ribs.

Why is the backbone so bendy?

Because it's not just one bone but 26 linked together like a chain. The top 24 bones are called **vertebrae** – seven in the neck, 12 in the back of the chest and five in the small of the back. Each vertebra is a solid block of bone, attached to its neighbour by a flexible joint consisting of a soft pad a bit like a rubber washer. These pads are the so-called **discs** that can cause so much pain if they burst or 'slip'. The discs allow the vertebrae to tilt slightly in any direction. If all the vertebrae are made to tilt forwards, the whole spine will bend forwards in a smooth curve. Acrobats, gymnasts and contortionists have amazingly bendy spines, because they are constantly exercising and stretching their back muscles.

By the way, the bottom two bones of your spine are also two of the bones in your bottom! There is the **sacrum** which is the central part of the **pelvis** and is attached to the hip bone on either side and below that is the tiny **coccyx** or tail-bone, less than 2.5 cm long – all that is left of our early animal ancestors' tail!

How is your head held up?

The heavy skull is balanced on the top of the spinal column rather like a beach ball balanced on the tip of your finger. It is kept in place by strong muscles which run from the spine to the skull, and which also move it in all directions when you look up, down or sideways.

What are ribs for?

You have 12 pairs of ribs attached to the 12 **chest vertebrae** of your spine. At the front the ribs are joined to a vertical **breast bone**. The whole structure is called the **rib-cage**. It has three main jobs:
1 It acts as bony armour protecting the organs in your chest and abdomen – heart, lungs, stomach, liver, kidneys etc.
2 When muscles raise and lower the rib-cage, it acts like bellows, sucking air in and blowing it out again (see Breathing page 26).
3 It is the main attachment for your arms and shoulders.

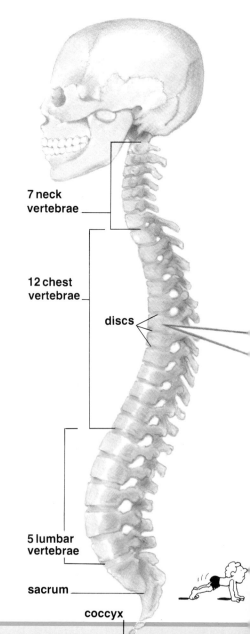

7 neck vertebrae

12 chest vertebrae

discs

5 lumbar vertebrae

sacrum

coccyx

What are shoulder-blades for?

Each of your arms is attached to a flat triangular bone or shoulder-blade. The shoulder-blade is connected to the bone of the upper arm by a ball-and-socket joint (see Hands and Arms page 32). Powerful muscles not only move the arm but also keep the flat shoulder-blade strapped down to the rib-cage. This arrangement makes the shoulder extremely flexible, able to move in all directions except backwards.

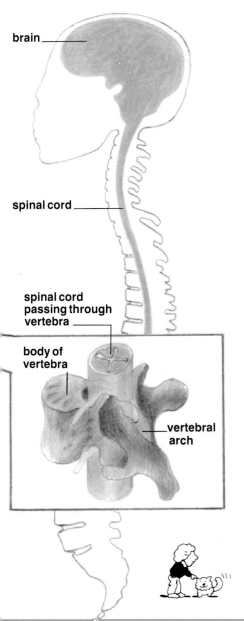

brain

spinal cord

spinal cord passing through vertebra

body of vertebra

vertebral arch

Reflex action

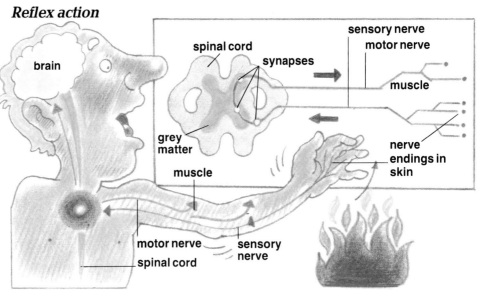

brain

spinal cord

synapses

grey matter

muscle

motor nerve

spinal cord

sensory nerve

sensory nerve
motor nerve

muscle

nerve endings in skin

What is the spinal cord?

It is the main 'trunk-route' for nerves to and from the brain. It stretches from the base of the brain, through a hole in the skull and down a channel through each of the vertebrae as far as about halfway down the back. All the way down the spinal cord there are pairs of large nerves branching off it and passing through little gaps between the vertebrae. These nerves send and receive signals to and from all parts of the body below the neck. Like the brain, (see page 14), the spinal cord consists of 'white matter' (nerve fibres) and 'grey matter' (nerve cells or **neurones**). Each nerve fibre is an incredibly long thread extending from a single nerve cell and connecting with a distant nerve cell in another part of the body. Because it contains grey matter, the spinal cord is really a long extension of the brain itself and these two parts of the nervous system are together called the **central nervous system** (see Body Systems page 6).

The spinal cord is constantly making very simple automatic decisions without 'consulting' the brain at all. For example, if your hand touches a hot plate, the pain detecting cells in the skin send signals along the nerves in your arm to the spinal cord. In the grey matter of the cord, relay nerve cells pass the signals to a set of nerve cells responsible for movement, which in turn signal to the arm muscles to pull your hand away from the hot plate. Ouch! This is known as a **reflex action** *and happens in a split second.*

Fascinating Facts

★ The tallest person ever was Robert Wadlow of Illinois USA who was 2.72 metres tall and still growing when he died in 1940 at the age of 22. The shortest mature person ever was Pauline Musters of Holland. She died of pneumonia aged 19 in 1895. She was just 59 cm tall.

Quiz

Complete the following sentence: Your tail-bone is called the

_ _ _ _ _ _ .

Tummy and Digestion

What goes on in the tummy?

A lot more besides gurglings and rumblings and tummy ache and feeling sick! Your tummy, or **abdomen**, contains your **stomach**, **liver**, **gall bladder**, **pancreas** and **intestines**. It is where your food is digested into simple chemical substances and absorbed into the bloodstream.

How does food get to the stomach?

By being squeezed down the **oesophagus** or food tube (see Throat page 24). Just inside the abdomen, the food tube joins the stomach, a muscular bag partly tucked under the rib cage.

Why are we sometimes sick?

It might be because we've eaten more than the stomach can deal with, or something that has irritated the stomach lining. There is actually a 'vomit centre' in the brain that receives signals from the eyes, nose, tongue, balance organs and also from the stomach itself. If the signals get strong enough, your tummy muscles twitch, and the contents are forced up the food tube and out of your mouth. Yuk! The sick tastes very sour because of the acid.

What causes burping?

Your stomach often gets air in it, from swallowing air or gas in fizzy drinks. If this is released suddenly, by opening the entrance valve, it vibrates in your throat, making a loud burp.

What happens in the stomach?

This is where your food is churned up and squidged about and thoroughly mixed with digestive juices. The stomach can stretch enough to hold a big meal of food and drink, plus digestive juices, up to about 1.5 litres worth. The stomach lining contains millions of special glands which produce the digestive juice. This is a mixture of **acid** and chemical substances called **enzymes**. These start to dissolve the food. For two to four hours after a meal, the muscular stomach mashes the food into a thick soupy liquid. The exit hole of the stomach now opens with each **peristaltic wave** (see Throat page 24) of the stomach wall and the liquid is squirted into the next part of the digestive system, the duodenum.

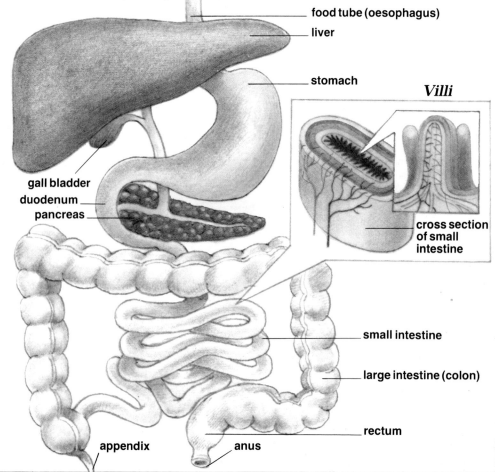

food tube (oesophagus)

liver

stomach

Villi

gall bladder
duodenum
pancreas

cross section of small intestine

small intestine

large intestine (colon)

rectum

appendix   anus

What happens to the food in the duodenum, and small intestine?

The duodenum is the first part of the **small intestine**. It is about 30 cm long and 2.5 cm wide and the rest of the small intestine is about 6.5 metres long. Not so small really! In the duodenum, more digestive juices are poured into the liquid remains of the food. Some come from the **pancreas**, a large gland which makes enzymes. The other juice poured into the duodenum is a green liquid called **bile**. It helps to digest fats by dissolving them. Bile is made in the **liver** and stored in a little muscular bag called the **gall-bladder**. Whenever you eat a fatty meal, bile is squirted into the duodenum like washing-up liquid. The small intestine is where simple chemicals that are useful to the body are absorbed into the bloodstream by oozing straight through the lining into a network of capillaries (tiny blood vessels) in the wall of the intestine, and then taken to the liver for chemical processing, storage or distribution round the body. This process of absorbing takes several hours and the food remains have to be kept moving (a bit like a production line in a factory) so the small intestine has to be 6.5 metres long to allow enough time.

The inner lining has a fluffy texture rather like velvet. This is because it is covered with millions of microscopic finger-like bumps called **villi**, which act like blotting paper, soaking up the useful chemicals. By the time the food remains reach the far end of the small intestine, they are made up of a thick paste of mainly indigestible material, which is then squeezed through a valve into the **large intestine**.

What happens in the large intestine?

The large intestine is much shorter than the small intestine. It's only about 1.8 metres long, but it is much wider (about 7.5 cm wide). Its other name is the **colon** or bowels. Millions of quite harmless bacteria help to break down the rest of the food remains, releasing water and minerals which are absorbed through the lining. As more and more water is removed, the remaining food waste becomes thicker and thicker. Pigments from the bile give it that brown colour. This waste is separated into small loads called **faeces**, which are passed out through the **anus** when you go to the lavatory.

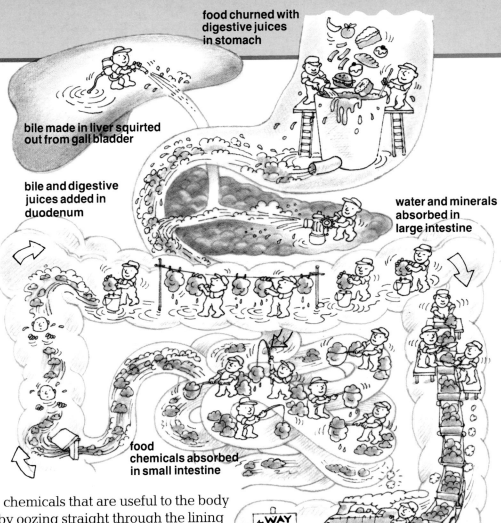

food churned with digestive juices in stomach

bile made in liver squirted out from gall bladder

bile and digestive juices added in duodenum

water and minerals absorbed in large intestine

food chemicals absorbed in small intestine

WAY OUT

waste is passed out through anus

·KENYON·

Fascinating Facts

★ During the course of a lifetime the average person eats nearly 30,000 kg of food. That's the equivalent of eating about six elephants (without the tusks!).

Quiz

It makes a green liquid (- - - - -)
It makes enzymes (- - - - - - - -)
It makes the stomach sour (- - - -)
They make a lining fluffy (- - - - -)

Waterworks

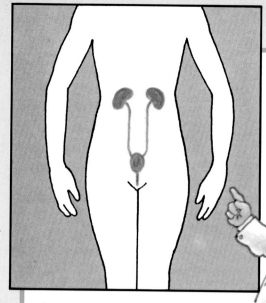

What are the waterworks?

The waterworks or **urinary system** (see Body Systems page 8) consists of the two kidneys, the bladder and the tubes connecting them. Their job is to filter unwanted substances from the blood, including any excess water.

Where are the kidneys?

They are at the back of the tummy or abdomen on either side of the spinal column, protected by the lower ribs. Each kidney is about 10 cm long and 6 cm wide.

How do the kidneys work?

In the cross-section shown, notice the three pipes attached to one edge of the kidney. These are:
1 An artery, taking blood to the kidney to be filtered.
2 A vein, taking filtered blood away.
3 A drainpipe for collecting the urine that results from the filtering and taking it to the bladder.

It has pinkish flesh and an odd-shaped cavity where the urine collects. The flesh consists of over a million filter units called **nephrons**.

Each nephron is a mini-tube, a few centimetres long, running from the outer part of the kidney, where the filter units are, to the collecting chamber on the inside. On its way

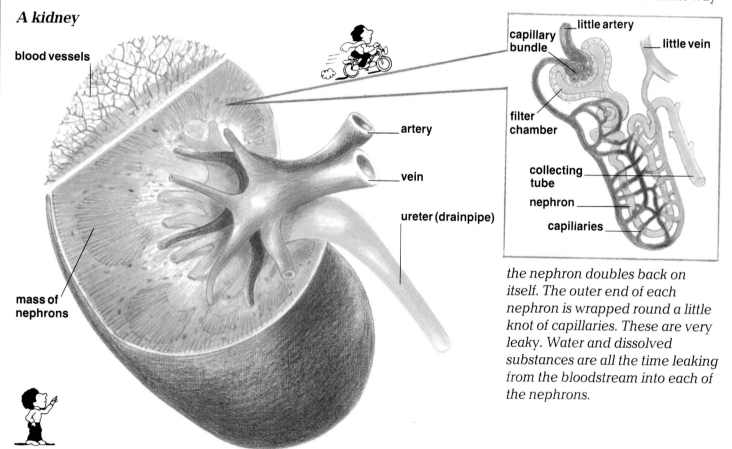

A kidney

the nephron doubles back on itself. The outer end of each nephron is wrapped round a little knot of capillaries. These are very leaky. Water and dissolved substances are all the time leaking from the bloodstream into each of the nephrons.

How much urine do the kidneys make in a day?

The average amount for an adult is about 1.5 litres. But it depends on how much you've drunk, because the more you drink, the more you urinate. In very hot weather you pass less urine as you lose a lot of water in your sweat (see Skin page 12).

From the kidneys, where does the urine go next?

*From each kidney, a drainpipe carries the urine down to the **bladder**. This is an elastic muscular bag where you store your urine until you are ready to urinate. As it fills with urine, it stretches like a balloon. With 200-300 ml in it, stretch-detectors in the bladder wall start to send signals to the brain, asking to be relieved at the earliest convenience. With about 500 ml in the bladder, you are desperately staggering around looking for somewhere, anywhere, to pee!*

Why is urine yellow?

There are a great many waste products and other substances dissolved in the water of urine which, if they were not got rid of, would poison our system. These include salt, and urea which is colourless, and a yellow substance which comes from bile in the liver (see Tummy page 36). It is this that makes urine yellow.

Every 24 hours the amount of water and waste substances filtered from the bloodstream by the kidneys is about 180 litres. That's about half a litre every five minutes! Luckily we are saved from spending our lives in the loo by the fact that 99% of the cleaned liquid goes back into the bloodstream in the kidneys. As the water is re-absorbed, the liquid left becomes more and more full of waste products. By the time it reaches the collecting chamber and drainpipe, it is a yellowish liquid – **urine**.

What happens when we pass water?

At the base of the bladder is an outlet which leads down a short pipe to the outside world. The outlet pipe, called the **urethra**, is about 3.5 cm long in women passing straight to a little hole near the front of the vulva (see Female Bits page 42). In men it emerges from the tip of the penis (see Male Bits page 40) and is up to 20 cm long.

Around the outlet pipe at the bottom of the bladder is a circular muscle called a **sphincter**. When this muscle is contracted (shortened) it pinches the pipe and shuts it off. When the muscle is relaxed the pipe opens and the urine flows out. Luckily we can control the action of our bladder sphincter and also the one around the **anus** (see Tummy page 36). But, unlike most muscles, whose normal position is relaxed, the sphincters' usual position is contracted and we have to decide when to relax them.

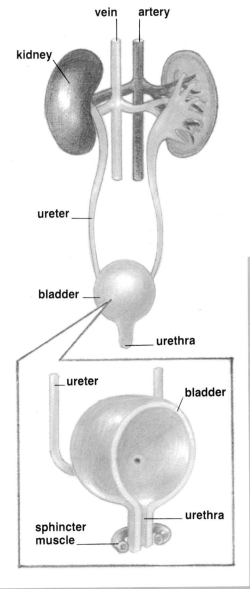

vein artery

kidney

ureter

bladder

urethra

ureter

bladder

sphincter muscle

urethra

Fascinating Facts

★ The average person passes about 41,000 litres of urine in their lifetime, enough to cover a full-size football pitch.

★ Nephrons were first discovered by Marcello Malpighi, a 17th century Italian scientist, using the recently invented microscope.

★ If you were to stretch out all the nephrons in both your kidneys and lay them end to end, they would stretch about 300 km.

Male Bits

What are the male bits and pieces for?

From the time of puberty onwards, a man's sex organs are designed to do just one thing – to produce male seed cells or **sperm** and put them into a woman's body as close as possible to the female egg cell, or **ovum**. All it takes is one sperm to combine with one ovum, and the result is a completely new human cell, which will then multiply and multiply until it becomes a new human being – a baby. This whole amazingly complicated process is called **sexual reproduction**. The sperm meeting the ovum is called **fertilisation**. The action of putting the sperm close to the ovum, by the man putting his **penis** into the woman's **vagina** is called **sexual intercourse** (see also Female Bits page 42 and Making a Baby page 44).

Male Bits

- bladder
- prostate gland
- penis
- urethra
- testicle
- scrotum
- anus

Testicles sliced to show tiny tubes

Sperm in the tubes

How does all this work?

*Let's start with the two balls or **testicles** in their little bag or pouch of skin called the **scrotum**. Each testicle is not round but oval and consists of a mass of microscopic tubes. These tubes are where the **sperm** are made.*

*As the millions of sperm come off the production line in the testicles, they are pushed into a long muscular tube which leads out of each testicle, passes up out of the scrotum and meets the other tube in a special gland at the base of the bladder. The gland makes a milky white liquid which is mixed with the sperm to produce the gooey fluid called **semen**.*

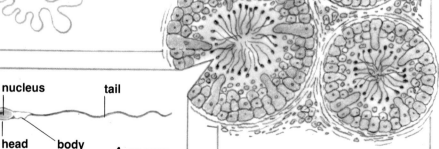

nucleus   tail

head   body   *A sperm*

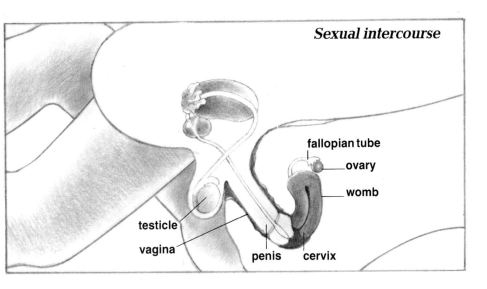

Sexual intercourse

fallopian tube
ovary
womb
testicle
vagina
penis
cervix

What does a sperm look like?

The male-seed cells, sperm, are just amazing. They can actually swim! They are microscopic tadpole-like creatures that seem to have a life of their own. They have a head, containing 23 chromosomes (the man's genetic instructions, giving all the information about him) which will combine with the 23 chromosomes in the female egg cell to form the 46 chromosomes that every cell in the new baby's body will have (see Body Basics page 4). The body of the sperm is an energy pack, and the tail thrashes about and propels the sperm forwards.

How do the sperm get into the vagina?

Just before sexual intercourse, as the man and woman begin to feel sexually excited, their sex organs change shape to prepare for the task ahead. The blood vessels in the man's penis swell and make the penis fill out and become stiff like a rod. When it is like this it is called an **erection** *and is ready to be put into the woman's vagina, which has also become firmer. During sexual intercourse a small amount of semen (about 3-4 ml) is squirted along the urinary outlet pipe and out at the end of the penis, into the vagina at its inner end.*

How far do the sperm have to swim?

Like frogmen commandos on an underwater raid, the sperm have to find the tiny entrance to the womb, swim through it to one of the fallopian tubes and swim along that until they find the egg. Altogether a journey of about 10 cm. To help them find their way the ovum gives off a chemical which acts as a sort of homing device, and the sperm swim towards it at about 1 cm a minute. Their biggest battle begins when they have found the egg since only one sperm can combine with the egg, and there is a mad scramble to be the winner. When one sperm has broken through the coating membrane that surrounds the ovum, the membrane turns instantly into a sort of armour plate, keeping the other sperms out. For the next instalment in the story of sperm and egg (see Making a Baby page 44).

Why do the male parts hang outside?

The reason is that sperm can only grow in cooler temperatures than the normal inside-body temperature.

What happens to boys at puberty?

Puberty is when your sex organs and body shape start to change into those of an adult. It is usually between the ages of 11 and 14. In boys, the first sign is usually a bit of hair appearing around the penis. Then the testicles start producing sperm, and the penis gets bigger. The whole body is now growing very fast and a boy's voice 'breaks' (see Throat page 24). Now boys become more muscular and hairy than girls, and by the end of their teens they are usually taller than girls of the same age. All these changes are 'switched on' by a special chemical or hormone in the blood (see Body Systems page 8).

Fascinating Facts

★ If you laid the tubes in the testicles end-to-end, there would be 1.6 km of tube.

★ Three to 4 ml of semen contains over 400 million sperm.

★ It would take about 40 sperm lying end-to-end to stretch across the head of a pin.

★ Sperm were discovered by the inventor of the microscope, Dutchman Antony van Leeuwenhoek, in 1677.

Female Bits

What are monthly 'periods'?

One of the first things that a girl notices when she reaches puberty, (usually at about 12-13 years), apart from her breasts growing, is some bleeding from the vagina. This can come as a bit of a shock but it is perfectly normal and natural. It is usually very slight, lasting a day or two, and then it stops until about 28 days later, when it happens again. This monthly happening is called the **menstrual period** or, because it can be a bit of a nuisance, 'the curse'.

Where exactly are the female bits and pieces?

*The female sex organs are all tucked away inside the lower abdomen. The only part that can be seen on the outside is the opening called the **vulva** protected on each side by two folds of skin called **labia**. Inside is the **vagina** the passage leading to the womb or **uterus**. The vagina is a muscular tube about 7-10 cm long pointing upwards and backwards. The womb is a triangular, muscular cavity shaped like an upturned flask. The neck of the womb or **cervix** is connected to the vagina by an opening no bigger than a pinhead. The other two points of the triangle are joined to the two **fallopian tubes**, one on each side. Each tube ends in a frilly opening which is wrapped around one of the two **ovaries** or egg factories.*

*The ovaries are about the same size as the testicles or sperm factories in males. But whilst the testicles make hundreds of millions of sperm every day, the ovaries make just one egg-cell or **ovum** a month.*

Why do periods happen every month?

Monthly periods happen because the ovaries start producing a ripe egg-cell every month. This is called **ovulation** and is under the control of the female hormones. When it happens, it starts a sort of time-switch which, about two weeks later, causes a period.

Female Bits

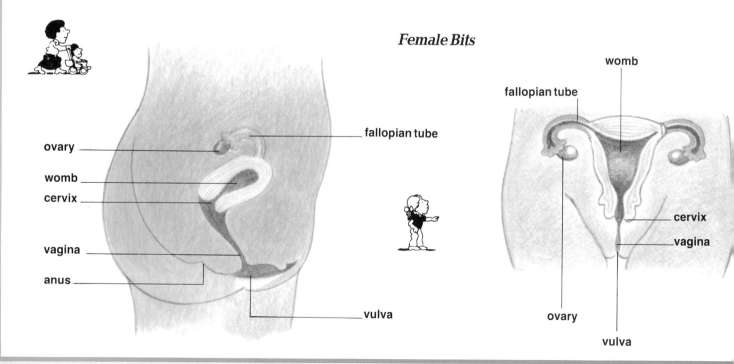

But what are periods for?

To answer that, let's see what happens to the ripe new ovum each month.

The ovum is a single very large cell, about half the size of a grain of salt. In ovulation it is released from the surface of one of the ovaries and is wafted into the nearby fallopian tube. It then begins a 3-4 day journey along the tube to the womb, pushed along by the rippling muscles in the tube wall.

When do periods stop?

If periods stop, it is usually the first sign of pregnancy, but they can sometimes stop for one month for some other reason such as a shock or upset. If a woman is over a week overdue or 'late', she should see her doctor.

There are no periods during pregnancy, and none when the breasts are making milk. So altogether, with each baby, a woman misses periods for about a year.

In middle-age, a woman's periods become less regular and eventually stop forever. This is because her ovaries are no longer producing ripe eggs. This marks the end of the time that she can have children and the change is called the **menopause**.

What is contraception?

This is the word which describes any of the methods for preventing pregnancy, to avoid having an unwanted baby. Examples are: the rubber **sheath** (worn by the man over his penis) which stops the sperm reaching the womb; 'the **pill**' which is taken by the woman and stops the ovaries making ripe eggs and the small plastic **coil**, put inside the womb to stop conception taking place.

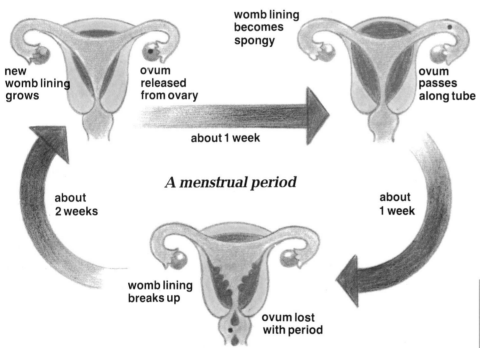

womb lining becomes spongy

new womb lining grows

ovum released from ovary

ovum passes along tube

about 1 week

A menstrual period

about 2 weeks

about 1 week

womb lining breaks up

ovum lost with period

*When the ovum is released each month, a special hormone is produced which makes the inner lining of the womb grow thicker and thicker, and spongier and spongier (see Hormone System, Body Systems page 8). In other words this gets the lining ready to lodge the ovum if it meets a merry band of sperm swimming along the tube from the womb end, and is **fertilised** by one of them. (See Male Bits page 40, and Making a Baby page 44). If the ovum*

becomes lodged, this is called **conception**. *However, if this does not happen within the next two weeks, a built-in time-switch turns off the production of the special hormone, and the spongy lining splits away from the wall of the womb. Over the next few days the womb expels the lining together with some blood, down the vagina. This is the period. About eight days after, the next ripe ovum is produced and the whole process starts again.*

Fascinating Facts

★ Each egg-cell or ovum is about 0.125 of a millimeter in diameter, just visible to the naked eye.

★ The average woman produces about 400 mature egg-cells in her lifetime. Fortunately most of them are not fertilised!

★ The record for the oldest mother goes to Ruth Kistler of Oregon USA who gave birth to a daughter in 1956 at the age of 57.

Making a Baby and Growth

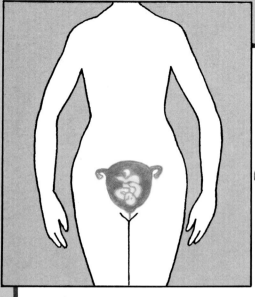

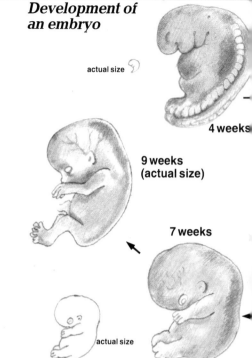

actual size

4 weeks

9 weeks (actual size)

7 weeks

actual size

How is a baby started?

*Every baby begins as one of the mother's eggs (ova), fertilised by one of the father's sperm (see Male Bits page 40). As the fertilised ovum continues its several days' journey through the fallopian tube towards the womb, it splits into two identical cells. Then each of these cells splits into two again and so on, making 8, 16, 32, 64 etc. It forms a hollow ball of cells which gets bigger and bigger, although really no bigger than a pinhead. By this time the ball (or **blastocyst**) is in the womb, nestling in the womb's spongy lining and digging some of its cells into the lining like roots. When it is firmly fixed it is **implanted** and the mother is pregnant.*

*Now some of the cells inside the blastocyst become gathered together in a sort of disc shape. This is the part which will eventually become the baby. It is called the **embryo**. The rest of the cells become the membrane surrounding the embryo in the womb. The part most deeply embedded in the lining becomes the embryo's life-support system the **placenta**.*

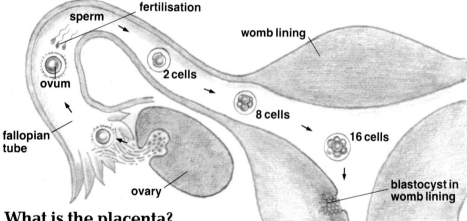

sperm — fertilisation

womb lining

ovum — 2 cells

8 cells

16 cells

fallopian tube

ovary

blastocyst in womb lining

What is the placenta?

When an astronaut goes for a space walk, he needs a life-support system to supply him with oxygen and other necessities for life in the emptiness of space. In a similar way, the baby which is developing in the liquid-filled space of the womb, cannot breathe air or eat food, so has to have a life-support system connecting it to its mother's bloodstream. This pad or placenta, develops its own tiny blood vessels which are connected to the embryo through a short stalk.

How does the embryo develop?

Week 1 A disc-shaped sandwich of cells the size of a pinhead.
Week 2 A sausage shape with a head and tail developing.
Week 3 A brain and heart begin to develop.
Week 4 The heart is beating.
Week 5 The face and limbs develop.
Week 6 Eyes, hands and the internal organs begin to take shape.
Week 7 The tail has gone and male and female bits begin to form.
Week 8 The ears are forming and it has webbed fingers and toes.
Week 9 It is fully formed with separate fingers and toes.

For the rest of the 38 weeks, or 9 months, of the pregnancy, the embryo (now called a **foetus**) just gets bigger and bigger, stretching the womb and giving the mother a very large bulge in the front of her tummy.